Lessons for
Climb Inside a Poem

Lessons for Climb Inside a Poem

Georgia Heard
Lester Laminack

HEINEMANN
Portsmouth, NH

firsthand
An imprint of Heinemann
361 Hanover Street
Portsmouth, NH 03801-3912
www.firsthand.heinemann.com

Offices and agents throughout the world

Climb Inside a Poem, Original Poems for Children
ISBN-10: 0-325-01721-2   ISBN-13: 978-0-325-01721-1

Lessons for Climb Inside a Poem
ISBN-10: 0-325-01722-0   ISBN-13: 978-0-325-01722-8

Reading and Writing Poetry Across the Year
ISBN-10: 0-325-01723-9   ISBN-13: 978-0-325-01723-5

Climb Inside a Poem full set
ISBN-10: 0-325-00983-X   ISBN-13: 978-0-325-00983-4

The authors and publisher wish to thank the following photographers who have generously given permission to use their portraits of the poets included in this volume:

Martin Benjamin (Joseph Bruchac)
Paul Lebel (Georgia Heard)
Jennifer Chen (Bobbi Katz)
Cheron Bayna (Pat Mora)
Linda Gallop (Marilyn Singer)
Anne Lindsay (Janet Wong)
Jason Stemple (Jane Yolen)

Original Illustrations by Terri Murphy in gouache on illustration board. Visit Terri at www.terrimurphyart.com

Library of Congress Cataloging-in-Publication Data on file at the Library of Congress.

Printed in the United States of America on acid-free paper

11 10 VP 2 3 4 5

Table of Contents

Lessons for
Climb Inside a Poem

INTRODUCTION to Lessons for Climb Inside a Poem

An Overview of *Climb Inside a Poem: Reading and Writing Poetry Across the Year*

Reading and writing poetry can support and extend young children's language and literacy development in many ways. *Climb Inside a Poem: Reading and Writing Poetry Across the Year* is a set of three components to help you incorporate poetry into your daily classroom routine:

- *Climb Inside a Poem* **big book:** Twenty-nine beautifully illustrated original poems written by some of our favorite children's poets. The poems are presented in a "big book" format, perfect for sharing with groups of children.

- *Lessons for Climb Inside a Poem*: A book of lessons to accompany each of the poems in the big book. These lessons will help children get up close and personal with poems—help them "climb inside" the poems and look around. The lesson book also includes a "Poet Profiles" section.

- *Reading and Writing Poetry Across the Year*: A guidebook offering a wide range of mini-lessons and activity suggestions to help you create a poetry-rich environment for children to inhabit, and to enrich their poetry reading and writing experiences all year long.

The *Climb Inside a Poem* Big Book

The 29 wonderful poems in the accompanying big book are written by some of the best contemporary children's poets writing today. Each poem offers just a tiny glimpse of a particular poet's work. If you or your children fall in love with a poem by a particular poet, take a look at the "Poet Profiles" section of the lesson book and explore more words and work by that poet.

You'll notice that there are a variety of poems in the *Climb Inside a Poem* big book. Some of the poems rhyme and have a strong rhythm and beat, but many use a variety of forms, styles, and craft techniques including metaphor, simile, and repetition. We believe that children will fall in love with all kinds of poetry if they have a chance to read or hear a variety of poems.

We've included 29 poems in the *Climb Inside a Poem* big book—one poem for almost every week of the school year. Instead of reading a new poem to students every day, we wanted to show how children can linger over one poem—climb inside and explore the many facets of one poem over the course of five days.

How to Use *Lessons for Climb Inside a Poem*

Living with a poem for one week is like spending time with a friend. At first, you might feel a little shy because the person is unfamiliar, but as the week progresses and you spend more time together, you discover that you understand each other, perhaps even have a lot in common, and you discover that the friendship has deepened.

Each poem in the big book is included in the lesson book as a reproducible for children to use and keep; feel free to use the Responding to the Poem page to invite kids to respond with their own writing or illustrations. The drawing on the Responding to the Poem page is the artist's original sketch for the art in the big book.

In addition to the reproducibles, there is one week's worth of lessons for each of the poems, a five-day lesson plan—Monday through Friday. Depending on the grade you teach and the poem itself, you might decide to use just the Monday and Tuesday lessons (the first two days), or you might introduce the poem on Monday and return to it later in the week. How you use the lessons is, of course, up to you. Ideally, you will spend five days getting to know one poem, and then move on to another.

Each week's structure is exactly the same. The idea behind the structure of the lessons is to invite children to climb inside the poem in different ways throughout the week. Of course, the structural themes in the five-day plans can be used for any poem—not just the poems in the big book. Here is the five-day lesson plan structure:

Monday: Introduce the Poem

The Heart of the Poem: On this first day, we suggest that teachers and children try to get to the "heart" of the poem, focusing on what the poem is about and any special features that the poem presents. In this section, we include an actual lesson that we've used with students as a way to introduce a particular poem.

Conversations About the Poem: We've written the actual language that can guide students in having a conversation about and around the poem. For some poems and with some classes, we've used the entire lesson; in other cases we've used just part of the lesson. The point is to get students talking with each other about a poem and how it relates to their lives. This is a way to personalize a poem, another way to "climb inside."

Tuesday and Wednesday: Ways to Climb Inside the Poem

In this section, we suggest two specific ways that you can invite children to "climb inside" the poem. There are a variety of activities and ways to get to know a poem better, including interactive writing, illustrating, acting, and choral reading.

Thursday: Poet's Talk

Another way to deepen understanding and extend exploration of a poem is to read what the poet says about writing poetry. In this section, we provide quotes and questions to get young poets talking with each other about what a poet says about writing poetry and how these words might be reflected in a particular poem. At the end of the lesson book, in the "Poet's Profiles" section, you'll find more about our featured poets, including photographs, biographical information, and some "poet-to-poet" advice for young poets.

Friday: Craft Talk

Every poem is built using poetic tools, and in this section, "Craft Talk," we highlight a few of the poem's specific craft features. You can discuss one craft feature of the poem or all of them, depending on your students' grade level and understanding of poetry. Sometimes we've highlighted punctuation and other conventions to help children realize that punctuation is an integral part of a poem's craft and meaning. Remember: craft is always at the service of the heart. When having "Craft Talk" with students, keep returning to the essential question: "How does this poetic tool help express the meaning and experience of the poem?"

A Note About Differentiation

Because *Climb Inside a Poem* will be read and used by teachers of different grade levels, we've included a variety of activities with varying levels of sophistication. Kindergarten teachers might want to introduce the poem, guide children in discussions, and perhaps choose one of the "Ways to Climb Inside the Poem" activities before moving on to another poem. Teachers of older children might want to spend more time exploring the craft of a particular poem.

Coordinating the Components

You can use the lessons in this book by themselves or in conjunction with the mini-lessons in the *Reading and Writing Poetry Across the Year* guidebook. Please refer to the guidebook for suggestions on how to use the components together throughout the year. These books are meant to support and inspire you and your students as you climb inside poetry—and we hope that you'll use them in any way that feels comfortable to you!

Poems

Where Do I Find Poetry?

I open my eyes and what do I see?
Poetry spinning all around me!

In small ants trailing over the ground,
bulldozing dry earth into cave and mound.

In a hundred grains of ocean sand
that I cradle in the palm of my hand.

In a lullaby of April rain,
tapping softly on my windowpane.

In trees dancing on a windy day,
when sky is wrinkled and elephant gray.

Poetry, poetry! Can be found
in, out, and all around.

But take a look inside your heart,
that's where a poem truly likes to start.

     — By Georgia Heard

Where Do I Find Poetry?

Georgia Heard

Monday: Introduce the Poem (big book pages 2 and 3)

The Heart of the Poem

Poetry can be found almost everywhere, if we just look around. Listen carefully to all of the places that this poet finds poetry. We'll talk about what you heard when I am done reading.

Conversations About the Poem

Were you surprised by where she looked? Turn and tell someone near you about some of the places where this poet found poetry.

Tuesday: Ways to Climb Inside the Poem

Interactive Writing

Asking children to answer the title question "Where Do I Find Poetry?" is a great invitation for them to begin thinking metaphorically and descriptively. It is hard to try to answer that question *without* discovering new ways of seeing things, because the idea of looking for poetry is all about looking closely at the world in all of its surprising specificity. At the top of a piece of chart paper, write the question "Where do we find poetry?" Referring back to the images in Georgia Heard's poem and reminding children that poets find their poetry in surprising nooks and crannies of the world, ask your students to answer the question. The resulting list of images is bound to be surprising and varied! You may choose to keep this chart available for children to add to during free times throughout the day; the structure of the poem affords room for infinite variation.

Wednesday: Ways to Climb Inside the Poem

Illustrating the Poem

Georgia Heard's poem is full of such specific and detailed images about where to find poetry that children will be easily inspired to illustrate the poem, and to add their own images to the mix. Give each of your students a piece of paper divided into several boxes, like a comic book or a storyboard. Ask them to hold the poem in their minds and to draw some of the images that struck them, one per box. Make sure to leave enough space for children to invent and draw their own images describing poetry's hiding places.

Thursday: Poet's Talk

Georgia Heard, the poet of "Where Do I Find Poetry?" says,

> **"Poetry is everywhere—especially surprising places— where most people wouldn't think of looking."**

Let's reread the poem and name places where poetry is found that are surprising or unusual. Have you ever found poetry in a place where most people wouldn't think of looking?

Friday: Craft Talk

- One way that this poem is unique is that it is about the act of writing poetry itself. This is a common and ancient technique called ***ars poetica***. Because writing poetry is such a reflective act, it can be wonderful for children to be invited to reflect on the act itself, in their own poems, just as this poet does.

- The poet uses strong and distinct **images** to paint surprising pictures in the readers' minds. This poem is a great example to use when you're asking your students to clarify the images in their own poems.

- The poet uses **metaphor** to describe the sky as "wrinkled and elephant gray." Children will be captivated by this description, and it is a wonderful example to use when asking children to use metaphor (or comparison) in their own poems.

Sky Wish

I wrote my wish
upon a kite;
closed my eyes,
grabbed its string—

through wind
I ran,
let it fly . . .

my wish came true.
It flew into
that wide, wide map
of sky.

— By Rebecca Kai Dotlich

Sky Wish
Rebecca Kai Dotlich

The Heart of the Poem

The speaker in the poem has written a wish on a kite. The poet never tells us exactly what the wish is—we get to guess! As I read, think about what that wish might be.

Conversations About the Poem

What do you think the speaker's wish was? Why do you think that? Turn and tell the person next to you.

The speaker's wish was that the kite would fly—but she could have chosen to fly a different wish up into the sky. If you were going to sail a wish up into the sky on a kite, what would you wish for?

Tuesday: Ways to Climb Inside the Poem

Acting

Ask the children to make a movie in their minds as they listen to you read the poem again. When you reach the end of the poem, have a brief conversation about the mind-pictures or images they saw in their minds as they listened. Turn those images into actions and create movements for each stanza. You might want to emphasize the strong action verbs in the poem to help create movements (verbs such as *wrote*, *closed*, and *grabbed*). The performance might go like this:

Poem	Action
I **wrote** my wish upon a kite;	Write in the air.
closed my eyes,	Close your eyes.
grabbed its string—	Reach up and close your fist.
through wind I **ran**, let it fly . . .	Run in place a few steps.
my wish came true. It **flew** into that wide, wide map of sky.	Stand still, looking up.

Wednesday: Ways to Climb Inside the Poem

Illustrating

Have ready a large, kite-shaped piece of paper or poster board. You may choose to have interested children decorate the "kite" during a free period. Cut strips of colored paper (enough for each child in your class). After rereading the poem, invite each child to write a wish on a slip of paper (remind students that these wishes will be hanging up, so they should choose a wish that is not private). Attach each wish to the tail of the kite (use string or ribbon for the tail), and hang it from your ceiling or in the hallway. You might place a container with extra strips of paper, pencils, and tape nearby so that visitors may add their wishes. Post "Sky Wish" nearby for inspiration.

Thursday: Poet's Talk

Let's see if Rebecca Kai Dotlich's words will give us a clue as to how she might have gotten the idea to write her poem "Sky Wish." She said,

"Find wonder in your world. Look—really look at that frog near the pond, that bus rumbling down the road, that sunflower towering over the fence, that puddle shimmering in the field, that tiny paper clip on the desk. Open your eyes and your heart to all the senses, all the imaginings, all the words and images in the world."

What do you think? Does this give us any hints as to where Rebecca Kai Dotlich maybe found the idea to write this poem? Let's remember her words, and when we're walking around in the world maybe we, too, can find wonder—to make our poems!

Friday: Craft Talk

◉ The poet uses **line breaks** and **white space** to help us figure out where we should pause. The white space might also help us picture the wide open space of the sky.

◉ The poet uses **metaphor** (or comparison) to describe the sky: "that wide, wide map of sky." The sky is not really a map, but the poet asks us to see it that way—this shows us a new way to look at the sky, and it helps us get a mind-picture of how the poet imagines the sky.

◉ The poet uses **strong verbs** (or action words) to create the images of movement.

◉ **Punctuation:** The poet uses a **dash** after *string* to keep us lingering before the next line. The poet uses **ellipses points** after *fly* to leave space for us to pause before the surprise of the next line.

Happy Toes

The waves say, "Whish, whish,"
and they chase our toes.
The waves curl up.
The waves splash down.
The waves say "Whish, whish,"
and they chase our toes.

Wet toes. Running toes.
And the wave goes
chasing, chasing, tickles
our happy toes.

    – By Pat Mora

Responding to the Poem

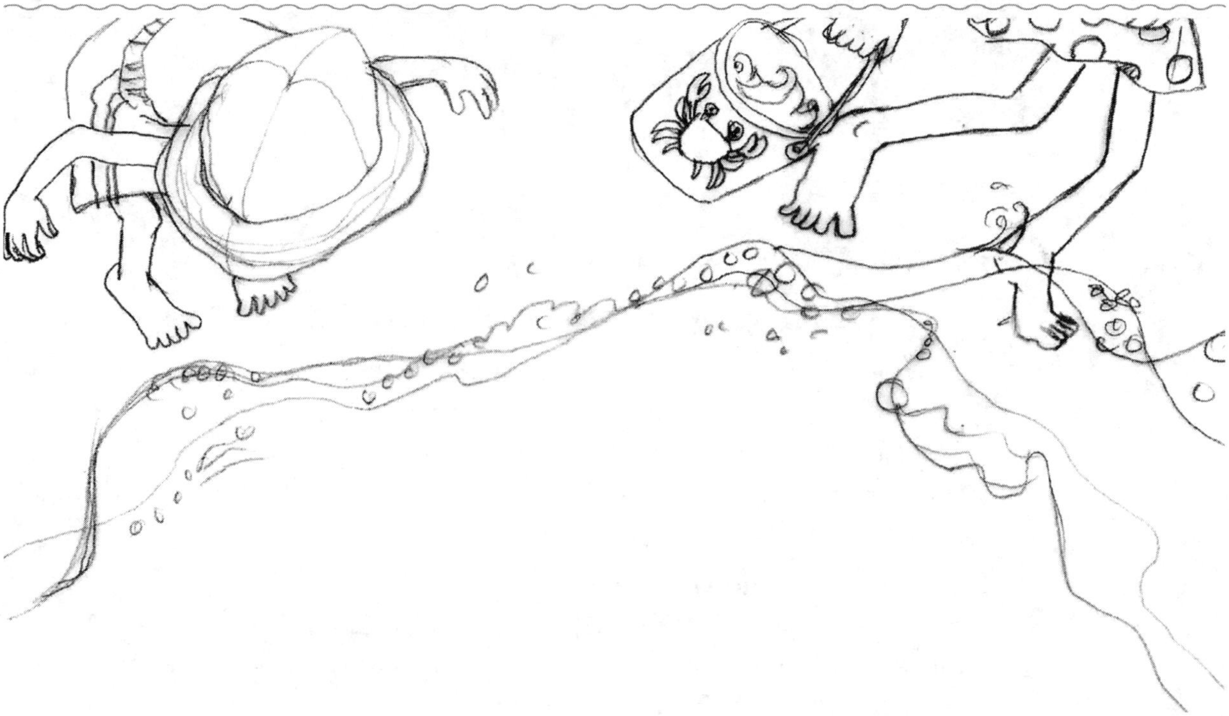

Happy Toes
Pat Mora

Monday: Introduce the Poem (big book page 5)

The Heart of the Poem

Have any of you been chased by a wave as you ran along the shore? I have—it definitely feels like the waves are alive and thinking about the best way to catch me! "Happy Toes" brings waves at the ocean to life as they chase the speaker's toes. The waves in Pat Mora's poem "Happy Toes" become the playmates of the child in the poem. She describes the waves so clearly we almost feel like we are there getting splashed too!

Conversations About the Poem

Sometimes poets bring things in their poems to life that aren't actually alive. For example, Pat Mora has the waves actually speak in "Happy Toes." Does anybody remember what the waves say to the speaker in this poem? Turn to the person sitting next to you and share.

The poet also tells us what the waves were doing. This clear description helps us to see and hear the waves' action. What did you see and hear the waves doing when I was reading? Turn and tell the person next to you what you remember.

Tuesday: Ways to Climb Inside the Poem

Choral Reading

Invite the children to accompany your reading of the poem by asking them to whisper the wave sounds while you read the poem out loud. They can repeat softly, "whish, whish," as if the waves are whispering in the background.

Acting

Read the poem and point out how the poet uses sound and action to help us see and hear the waves. When you reach those images, pause to create a motion to accompany the phrase. Let children invent their own actions and movements to accompany the poem. Try acting out the poem in several different ways using both choral reading and movement. Here is an example:

Poem	Action
The waves say, "Whish, whish," and they chase our toes.	Lean in and repeat "whish, whish" in a whisper while letting your fingers scurry across the tabletop.
The waves curl up. The waves splash down.	Slowly extend your arms with palms up; "curl" your fingers and hands toward you while slowly raising your forearms. Drop your arms and hands palms down in a "splash."

Poem	Action
The waves say, "Whish, whish," and they chase our toes.	Lean in and repeat "whish, whish" in a whisper while letting your fingers scurry across the tabletop.
Wet toes. Running toes. And the wave goes	Continue with fingers scurrying.
chasing, chasing, tickles our happy toes.	Make giggling sounds.

Wednesday: Ways to Climb Inside the Poem

Interactive Writing

Many poets write poems that bring the natural world to life. Brainstorm a list of elements of the natural world (thunder, wind, and so on). Choose one and use it as the subject of a poem using **personification**. If you choose the wind, for example, ask the children to come up with a repeating line that describes what the wind says, as Pat Mora does for the waves. Then ask the children to think of specific physical movements that describe the subject—for example, not just "the wind blows," but "the wind skips and dances." Intersperse the repeating line in the physical description, as Mora does.

Thursday: Poet's Talk

Pat Mora, the poet of "Happy Toes," says,

> "We are all poets, and each of us has songs or rhymes or stories or word pictures that we can share."

I'm wondering if all of you here know that you're poets. What do you think? Do you consider yourselves poets? Turn to someone next to you, and share your thoughts about what Pat Mora said.

Friday: Craft Talk

- The poet repeats "The waves" to begin four lines. She also repeats the beginning two lines to end the first stanza. And she repeats several other words. Many poets use **repetition** to add music to their poems. Maybe the repeating words and lines in this poem are like the ocean waves, which repeat as they roll up on the shore.

- **Punctuation:** The poet uses "speaking marks," or **quotation marks**, to show what the waves are saying.

- The poet uses **personification** to bring the waves to life; they talk, chase, and tickle just like a human would. Children often enjoy writing about inanimate objects as if they were alive.

Dear Friend in the Desert

Today, I am sending you
a jar of my ocean.
Pour it into your teacup

so you can smell the salty air,
hear waves crash,
feel the sand
between your toes.

Fill your teacup full of sea,
then, please, *please*,
come visit me.

— By Kristine O'Connell George

Dear Friend in the Desert
Kristine O'Connell George

Monday: Introduce the Poem (big book page 6)

The Heart of the Poem

Kristine O'Connell George's poem is written like a letter to a faraway friend. There is a name for this kind of poem: an apostrophe poem. Lots of poets have written poems that could be read as letters to one specific person. You can tell how far apart the speaker and her friend live and how much the speaker misses her friend.

Conversations About the Poem

I got the feeling that the speaker hasn't seen her friend for a long time, and she really misses her. What is she sending to her friend along with the letter? Why do you suppose that she is sending a jar of seawater to her desert friend?

Are there people in your lives whom you love very much who are far away from you? What could you send them that would remind them of you and of where you live?

Tuesday: Ways to Climb Inside the Poem

Writing/Illustrating

As Kristine O'Connell George shows us, letters can be poems, too. Have your students each think of someone they like or love who is far away to whom they could write an **apostrophe poem**. Have them write "Dear_____" at the top of their paper as a title. If you are working with less experienced poets, you may want to have them set up their poems as list poems, repeating and completing a phrase, for example, "I miss . . ." More sophisticated young poets will be able to use "Dear Friend in the Desert" as a model and will not need as much structure to write their own poems. You may choose to have your students illustrate their poems and to actually mail them off to their loved ones.

Wednesday: Ways to Climb Inside the Poem

Interactive Writing

The poet imagines that the speaker, who lives by the sea, is sending her dear friend who lives in the desert, a jar of seawater to make the distance between them seem not so great. If your class has a pen-pal class, this is a great opportunity to write a poem-letter about what your children might send to them. If you have no pen-pal class, you may choose an imaginary class to write to ("Dear Kindergartners in China," for example). The idea is to ask your children to think about what typifies the town or neighborhood surrounding their school, and what they might "send" to someone that would give a sense of where they are from. Invite them to think beyond literal things to send; for example, they might send "the sound of the subway underneath the sidewalk on the way to school" or "the curious squirrel that looks in our window when we are reading." Providing children with a few such examples will give them a boost into thinking this way. The result will be a lovely list poem describing their neighborhood. It's even better if they actually have a class to send a copy to!

Thursday: Poet's Talk

Kristine O'Connell George, the poet of "Dear Friend in the Desert," says,

> "Many of my poems are about things I love so much that I feel
> I have to write about them."

When you listened to her poem, did you feel that she loved her friend so much that maybe she had to write about her friend in the poem? Have you ever felt that way? Turn and talk to the person next to you. Tell about a time that you loved something or someone so much that you had to write about it, or tell about something or someone you love so much that you could write about it.

Friday: Craft Talk

- The poet uses the **letter** or **apostrophe poem** to make her poem feel very personal; we get to hear what she wants to say to her friend. Children will be able to relate to the idea of missing someone far away, and they will also easily be able to try out this simple form.

- The poet uses strong **images** to describe how the "teacup full of sea" will remind the desert friend of the seaside and of her friend who lives there.

Tooth Truth

This is the truth.
I am sick of this tooth.

The wiggling.
The waggling.

Oh, what a pain.

Oops!

What just happened?

It is hard to explain.

My tooth
just
fell out
in my bowl
of
chow mein.

— By Lee Bennett Hopkins

Tooth Truth
Lee Bennett Hopkins

Monday: Introduce the Poem (big book page 7)

The Heart of the Poem
Sometimes poets like to surprise us at the end of a poem, as Lee Bennett Hopkins does in "Tooth Truth." Let me see a thumbs-up if you have lost a tooth, or if you have a wiggly tooth right now. You never know when or how those teeth are going to fall out—it's always sort of a surprise, just like it is for the speaker in this poem!

Conversations About the Poem
Were you surprised at the end of the poem by where the speaker's tooth ended up? Have you ever been surprised by how or when one of your teeth fell out? Turn and tell someone near you about what happened.

Tuesday: Ways to Climb Inside the Poem

Acting
Read the poem aloud and pause after each stanza to create a set of gestures to accompany the words. For example, try these actions:

Poem	Actions
This is the truth.	Hands open. Palms up with fingers spread.
I am sick of this tooth.	Exasperated expression on your face.
The wiggling.	Exaggerate wiggling motion with your right hand,
The waggling.	your index finger on one tooth.
	Repeat with left hand.
Oh, what a pain.	Hands open, palms on cheeks.
Oops!	Eyes open wide.
What just happened?	Mouth open as if saying, "Oh."
It is hard to explain.	Look downward as if
My tooth	staring into a bowl.
just	
fell out	Place one hand over your mouth.
in my bowl	
of	
chow mein.	Eyes open wide as if in surprise.

Wednesday: Ways to Climb Inside the Poem

Interactive Writing

The early years of schooling are the years when tooth-losing is frequent and magical. Almost every child in the primary grades has lost at least one tooth (or has heard an earful about tooth-losing from friends and siblings), so writing a "lost tooth" poem together draws on your students' shared life experience, which is always a good place to start a shared writing experience. One element of Lee Bennett Hopkins's poem to focus on might be the short list of how the loose tooth moves before it falls out ("The wiggling. / The waggling."). You might begin by asking children to think of a list of words that describe how a loose tooth moves; encourage them to make up words, too, if you feel comfortable. You might then go back to your list and make a sentence that includes each wiggly word. This gives children great practice in thinking of many specific verbs for one type of motion and then incorporating those words into a poem.

Thursday: Poet's Talk

Lee Bennett Hopkins writes about how he gets ideas for his poems,

> "Something inside my head seems to say: 'Write a poem about me! I need attention!'"

When we read his poem "Tooth Truth," can we make a guess about what needed attention when he wrote this poem? Turn to the person next to you and share your guess.

Friday: Craft Talk

◉ The poet uses the **white space** and **line breaks** to suggest the pace and tone. Slowing the pace by writing very few words per line helps us slow down as we read the poem. The pace mimics the slow, back-and-forth wiggle of a loose tooth!

◉ The poet uses **specific verbs** to describe the action of a wiggling tooth. Young poets can easily be encouraged to choose more descriptive action words in their own poems.

◉ **Print Conventions:** The poet shows emphasis with the use of **italics** on the word *Oops*.

◉ The poet uses a **surprise ending**—who knew that loose tooth would fall out in the speaker's dinner? You may ask young poets to notice surprise endings in other poems or to try adding their own surprises at the ends of poems they write themselves.

Quack, Quack

Mother duck

leads her ducklings

across the pond.

One duckling, uno, QUACK,

Two ducklings, dos, QUACK, QUACK,

Three ducklings, tres,

QUACK, QUACK, QUACK.

Four ducklings paddling in the sun.

QUACK, QUACK, QUACK, QUACK.

— By Pat Mora

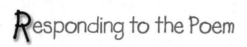

Quack, Quack
Pat Mora

Monday: Introduce the Poem (big book page 8)

The Heart of the Poem

Sometimes poets play around with the sounds of words in their poems, or the sounds that things in their poems make, just like Pat Mora does in her poem "Quack, Quack" about a group of ducklings paddling by. Even if you've never seen or heard a duck family, this poem will make you feel like you are right there with them, in the middle of all of their quacking! You'll also hear some Spanish words in the poem—keep your ears open!

Conversations About the Poem

So, what did you hear? Have you ever seen a duck family traveling together? How did the sounds in this poem remind you of that experience?

Why do you suppose Pat Mora uses Spanish numbers in her poem along with English numbers?

Tuesday: Ways to Climb Inside the Poem

Acting

Children, especially kindergartners, will delight in taking turns acting out this poem. The poem defines the actors' roles clearly, and simply reading the poem aloud provides stage directions for your actors! Choose children to be the mother duck and each of the four ducklings. Sit the rest of the class in a circle around your rug. As you read, instruct the actors to "paddle" off in a line across the "pond." Have the actors speak the "QUACK" sounds. Because this is likely to be a very popular activity, and because it goes very quickly, you may want to act it out several times, allowing different children to be the actors.

Wednesday: Ways to Climb Inside the Poem

Interactive Writing

Children love animal poems like this one. Choose an animal that is familiar to all of your students—one that they see every day in the neighborhood around your school, or one that they might have seen recently on a class trip (perhaps to the zoo). Ask the children to think of the sounds that the animal makes, and build a poem together around those sounds, as Pat Mora does in her poem "Quack, Quack." Depending on your class, you may choose to rely more or less heavily on the structure of Mora's poem to guide you. Children will enjoy acting out the poem you create together as much as they will enjoy acting out "Quack, Quack."

Thursday: Poet's Talk

Pat Mora, the poet who wrote "Quack, Quack," was born in El Paso, Texas, which is on the border of Mexico. She grew up speaking both Spanish and English in her home. Writers' lives shape the poems and stories they write. How does Pat Mora's poem "Quack, Quack" give us a little window into her life? Turn to someone near you, and share what you think.

Friday: Craft Talk

- The poet uses the **white space** and **line breaks** to suggest the pace and tone, as well as to visually mimic the poem's content. The children will notice how the shape of the poem changes (broadens) as more ducklings join the mix.

- The poet uses **onomatopoeia**, or **sound words**, to describe her subject. Children will love thinking of other animals and their sounds, and making their own poems!

- **Print Conventions:** Pat Mora uses **capital letters** for the sound of the ducks. This encourages us to say those words a little louder than the rest of the poem.

Why?
Why?
Why?

"Why are rocks so hard?
Why is the sun so hot?

Why do flowers have different colors?
Why do ponies trot?

Why do trees lose leaves in the autumn?
Why are bears so very furry?

You can answer when you can.

I am never in a hurry."

— By Lee Bennett Hopkins

Why? Why? Why?

Lee Bennett Hopkins

Monday: Introduce the Poem (big book page 9)

The Heart of the Poem

This poem reminds me of all of you, because it asks big questions about the way the world works—just like you do. We might think that poems have to tell us the answers to everything instead of just asking, but sometimes just asking questions makes a poem. Listen as I read, and then we'll talk about the questions.

Conversations About the Poem

The speaker in this poem is asking questions about the world that can't be easily answered, if they can be answered at all. We all wonder things about the world we live in. Some questions have clear answers that you can find by reading books or asking an expert, such as, "How do seeds grow?" Some questions don't have clear answers, but just asking them helps us think about our amazing and mysterious world—questions like, "Will time ever end?" Have you ever wondered about the same things that the poet asks in this poem? What are some of your questions about the world? Turn and tell someone near you what you wonder.

Tuesday: Ways to Climb Inside the Poem

Illustrating

Sometimes the answers we try to give to our big questions about the world can become poems. Read through the poem again and invite the children to choose one of the questions. Have them write and illustrate (or just illustrate, if they are not yet writing independently) their own answer (stress to your students that this can be a poetic answer rather than a purely scientific one). Or you may choose to invite children to ask and answer a question of their own. Have various materials available: paper, paint, colored pencils, crayons, images from magazines, fabric scraps, glue, and so on. Some children may want to draw or paint, and others may wish to make a textured collage or a three-dimensional object. The art could be displayed in a "gallery of questions and answers."

Wednesday: Ways to Climb Inside the Poem

Reading the Poem as a Round

Divide the class into three groups for reading the poem as a round. Group 1 will start reading the poem and keep reading until the end of the poem. When Group 1 says the word "trot" in the 4th line, that will be Group 2's cue to begin reading the poem to the end. When Group 2 says the word "trot," that will be Group 3's cue to begin reading the poem to the end. It might be helpful to copy the poem so everyone in the class can hold their own copy as they read. The reading may sound chaotic at first, but listen to the chorus of questions. The round will end with Group 3 reading the last two lines alone.

Thursday: Poet's Talk

Lee Bennett Hopkins says,

"The best part about writing poetry is . . . trying to pare down thoughts in a few—but wonderfully, magically, chosen—words."

You've probably noticed that poems usually have fewer words than stories do—so every word has to be carefully chosen because there are not that many of them. Let's read, "Why? Why? Why?" again, and take a look at the wonderful and magical words that Lee Bennett Hopkins chose for this poem.

Friday: Craft Talk

- The poet provides an example of how simply asking **questions** about things we don't understand can make a poem.

- The poet uses **repetition** as he asks questions in the poem. All the questions begin in a similar way: "Why . . . ?"

- The poet chooses to use **rhyme** to reinforce the musical rhythm of the poem, but not all of the end-words rhyme. See if your class can hear the words that rhyme.

- **Punctuation:** The poet uses **question marks** to show that every line is a question except for the last two lines.

Who's Coming to Tea?

Anna's brought Tillie

Her brown teddy bear.

Molly's got Rabbit

Who's really a hare.

Ali's arrived with

An owl in backpack.

Caitlin has brought her old Pooh

In a black sack.

Maddison's come with a doll

And doll gear,

So everyone asked to the party

Is here.

We're ready to start.

But . . . Wait. Oh, please wait.
There's somebody standing
Outside at the gate.
It's Michael and Nicky,
With toys in a tin.
Open the gate, boys,
And come right on in.

— By Jane Yolen

Who's Coming to Tea?

Jane Yolen

Monday: Introduce the Poem (big book pages 10 and 11)

The Heart of the Poem

Sometimes poets use lists to give readers lots of details all at once. In this poem, we hear a list of people and toys that are coming to a tea party. Some people might think that tea parties are only for girls—but this poem surprises us. As I read it, you will hear about all the girls who were invited. Each of them brings a stuffed animal or a doll along. But at the end, some unexpected visitors show up. Listen now as I read this aloud one time through. Who are the unexpected visitors?

Conversations About the Poem

Let's look again at this poem and think about how the poet let us know the boys were surprise visitors to the tea party. How do we know they weren't invited? Can you tell if the girls were glad to see the boys arrive? What in the poem makes you think that?

Tuesday: Ways to Climb Inside the Poem

Choral Reading

Read the poem once through as a model for the students. Then divide the class into five groups: one group assigned to each girl's name. Each group will read as the appropriate girl's name is featured. Have all voices join together on the line beginning "So everyone asked to the party. . . ."

Illustrating

Ask your students who they would invite to a tea party. Remind them that all different kinds of people (and their toys!) can enjoy a tea party. If your students are writing independently, you may ask them to write a list of the loved ones and toys that are coming and then draw a picture. If they are not yet writers, ask them to envision their tea party and draw a picture using as much detail as possible showing who is there. Then read the poem out loud, and ask everyone to show their drawing to everyone in the class.

Wednesday: Ways to Climb Inside the Poem

Interactive Writing

The poem is put together as a simple list of the children arriving at the tea party with their toys. Children tend to love making lists in general. Write a list poem about having a tea party in the class, using the names of each of the students and asking them what stuffed animal or toy they would bring to the class tea party. Write their answers on chart paper in a list poem format—and try to come up with a surprise ending of who might show up unexpectedly.

Thursday: Poet's Talk

Jane Yolen, the poet of "Who's Coming to Tea?" says,

> "Sometimes a line runs through my head 'Oh, world, I wish . . .' and a poem comes from that."

Do you think that this poem might have started this way, with a wish for something? What do you think her wish might have been?

Friday: Craft Talk

- **Specific detail** is used to help the reader visualize and imagine the event as if it were real. For example, "Anna's brought Tillie / Her brown teddy bear" clearly describes what kind of toy Tillie is and what she looks like. Point out other examples of specificity, and help your writers recognize the importance of details in writing.

- The poet uses **proper names** to refer to the children in the poem—using the names Anna, Molly, Ali, Caitlin, Maddison, Michael, and Nicky adds specificity to the world of the poem. Children can be encouraged to use proper names in their own poetry as well.

- **Punctuation:** An **ellipsis** is used in only one place—"But . . . Wait. Oh, please wait." Here it slows the reader, gives us pause, and draws attention to the repeated "wait" at the end of the line.

Making Soup

Soup, soup, we're making soup
    with grass and stones and mud (one scoop),
        a hunk of cheese, a celery stalk,
        an old cigar, a piece of chalk.
We stir it with a ballpoint pen,
    then throw it out and start again.

    – By Marilyn Singer

Making Soup
Marilyn Singer

Monday: Introduce the Poem (big book page 12)

The Heart of the Poem
This poem's title, "Making Soup," made me think at first that Marilyn Singer was going to be writing about real soup, the kind you eat. But then as I read, I changed my mind. Listen as I read it aloud, and see what you notice about this special soup!

Conversations About the Poem
What did the speaker in the poem put in the soup? Where in the poem did you realize that the soup was pretend? Have any of you ever made a pretend soup or mud pies or other kinds of made-up food like this? Turn and tell your neighbor about what you did.

Tuesday: Ways to Climb Inside the Poem

Choral Reading
Read the poem aloud and emphasize the rhythm in each line. Pat that rhythm on your thighs and invite the children to repeat after you. Then read one line at a time as you pat out the rhythm. Continue reading with the rhythm, adding one line at a time until the children can pat the rhythm and read it with you all the way through.

Acting
Now say the poem all together and act it out: stirring the soup in line 1; adding the ingredients in lines 2–4; stirring in line 5; and throwing out and starting again in line 6. You might even want to bring in a big bowl, or use a hat or another container, and ask children to draw the ingredients and cut them out to stir into their imaginary soup.

Wednesday: Ways to Climb Inside the Poem

Interactive Writing
Marilyn Singer's poem is structured much like a real recipe, with a list of ingredients and then some instructions for what to do with them. You can use this structure to create a collaborative recipe poem of your own.

Brainstorm a list of pretend recipe ideas. Will your class write about making soup, too? Or pie? Or pancakes? Choose an idea and write it at the top of your chart paper. You may want to give the students a boost into the poem by borrowing the line "Soup, soup, we're making soup," from Marilyn Singer and substituting the students' choice of food. Tell your students that often poems are made of lists—sort of like a real recipe lists ingredients. Have your students list ingredients for their pretend recipe. When you feel you've collected enough ingredients, have the students come up with a few quick instructions for how to put the ingredients together. Encourage your students to be inventive—remind them that this is a poetry recipe, not a real one!

Thursday: Poet's Talk

The poet Marilyn Singer says,

"Listen to words and sentences. What kind of music do they have? How is the music of poetry different from the music of songs?"

I'm going to read her poem "Making Soup" to you again, and let's ask ourselves Marilyn Singer's questions: "What kind of music does the poem have? How is the music of poetry different from the music of songs?"

Friday: Craft Talk

- **Rhythm** is created in this poem by the careful placement and balance of syllables and stress. As you read, you will be able to tap out or clap a rhythm. This is something that young children can easily be taught to notice in other people's poems. Very sophisticated young writers may be able to consciously try out rhythmic structures in their own poems.

- Paying attention to the poem's **line breaks** and **white space** as we read helps us to set the pace.

- This poem relies on a **list** of ingredients—much as a real recipe does. In this case, the list adds detail and strengthens the poem's rhythm.

- The poet uses the "we" **point of view** in this poem, giving the reader a sense of being included in the action.

- **Punctuation:** The poet puts **parentheses** around "one scoop" as if the speaker is talking to us as an aside.

How I Hopscotch

I scratch the chalk,
mark the walk,
square the box,
cross the hatch.

Knock the door,
get a friend,

toss the rock,
hop the scotch,
bottom to top,
top to bottom,
    hip *hop* skip *skop*
    hop hop hop!

        – By Kristine O'Connell George

How I Hopscotch
Kristine O'Connell George

Monday: Introduce the Poem (big book page 13)

The Heart of the Poem

Has anybody ever played the game of hopscotch? Show us how. In this poem, the poet describes in rhythmic words a game of hopscotch. The sound and rhythm of the words in the poem remind me of the sound and rhythm of an actual game of hopscotch. As I read, listen to how the poem might teach us to play hopscotch.

Conversations About the Poem

Does anyone remember the first things the speaker does to play a game of hopscotch? Let's reread the first stanza to see. What does the next part or stanza tell us? Let's reread the second stanza. The speaker has drawn the game on the sidewalk, and now he or she knocks on a friend's door. What does the third part, or stanza, tell us?

Tuesday: Ways to Climb Inside the Poem

Acting

The poem's directions for how to play hopscotch are so clear that your class can follow them and act out the poem together. You might want to point out how the **strong verbs** (or action words) can help children create movement. If you have access to a blacktop area or sidewalk where your class can actually play hopscotch while reading the poem, that's even better!

Poem	Actions
I **scratch** the chalk, **mark** the walk,	Make movements of writing on a sidewalk.
square the box, **cross** the hatch.	This time, make the shape of a box as you act out writing on a sidewalk.
Knock the door, get a friend,	Pretend to knock on a door. Pretend to greet a friend.
toss the rock, **hop** the scotch, bottom to top,	Toss a pretend rock. Stand on one leg and hop.
top to bottom, hip *hop* skip *skop* *hop hop hop!*	Keep hopping on one leg. Hop to the rhythm of the words.

Wednesday: Ways to Climb Inside the Poem

Choral Reading

This poem has such a strong rhythm that it invites a chant-like reading that mimics the rhythm of playing the game. Divide the class into two groups. Have Group 1 read the odd lines, Group 2 the even lines. Close with all voices reading the final two lines.

Rhythmic Reading

After the class has read the poem a few times as a choral reading, shift attention to the rhythm with movement. For example: Pat your thighs once as you say "I." Clap three times, once on each word, as you say "scratch the chalk." Pat your thighs once as you pause at the end of the line. As you continue to read, clap on each word and pat your thighs once on each pause. For the last two lines, increase the pace slightly and clap on each word.

Thursday: Poet's Talk

Kristine O'Connell George says,

"There's a certain private joy in finding an image or a handful of words that perfectly captures what I want to say."

When she says "a handful of words," I can't help but think about the wonderful words she used in her poem "How I Hopscotch." If you could pick just a few words from this poem, what would be your favorites? Has that ever happened to anyone here, that you found "a handful of words" that "perfectly captured" what you wanted to say?

Friday: Craft Talk

- Much of the poem's rhythm is created by the **sounds** of the words—*chalk, walk, box, hatch,* and so on. These short, clear words mimic the short bumps and jumps of an actual game of hopscotch.

- The poet uses **strong verbs** to begin almost every line. Highlight the verbs, and suggest that they give the poem a feeling of action.

When I Ride My Bike

I carry the wind
In my shirt and hair—
Wind and I go everywhere.
With wind at my back
I coast and glide—
(Wind whistles his thanks
For the piggyback ride.)

I wheel around—
Wind's on the attack!
I stand up and pump
And fight right back.
Wind, my friend and my enemy—
When I ride my bike
It's just you and me!

— By Patricia Hubbell

When I Ride My Bike

Patricia Hubbell

Monday: Introduce the Poem (big book page 14)

The Heart of the Poem

Have you ever felt a really strong wind blow when you're outside riding a scooter, skating, riding a bike, or even just running? In this poem, the poet gives the wind its own personality—sometimes a friendly personality, and sometimes not so friendly! As you listen, close your eyes and pretend you're riding a bike on a windy day—can you feel the wind helping you go faster? As you turn around, can you feel it pushing you back?

Conversations About the Poem

Turn and talk with a neighbor about how the wind can be a friend or an enemy on a windy day. Do you notice a difference when you are riding or walking with the wind blowing in your face? How about when the wind is blowing from behind you?

Tuesday: Ways to Climb Inside the Poem

Choral Reading

Read the poem once through as a model for the students. Be sure that you use your voice to demonstrate a shift in tone between the two stanzas. For example, the first stanza portrays the wind as a playful friend so the tone is playful and light. Yet, in the second stanza the wind is portrayed as more of an adversary, and the tone is more of a struggle, more stressful. In those places where the stress increases, let your voice become more strained or a bit louder. Let children hear the shift in pacing, tone, intensity, and mood as the wind shifts. Then have them read chorally with you, shifting their voices to reflect the tone in each stanza.

(For stronger readers) Divide the class into two groups facing in opposite directions. Each group reads one stanza.

Acting

Invite the children to pantomime the action in "When I Ride My Bike" as you read the poem aloud. In the first stanza, when the wind is portrayed as a friend, children can make soft, gentle wind sounds while you read the poem aloud. In the second stanza, children can make louder, more fierce wind sounds while you read the poem aloud.

(To make this very realistic, you may want to turn on a fan and let it blow from behind the group during the first stanza. Let them feel the breeze at their backs to experience the imagery more completely. For the second stanza, have everyone turn and face the opposite direction. Now the wind will be blowing at them as you read the second stanza!)

Wednesday: Ways to Climb Inside the Poem

Illustrating

You'll need 3″ × 5″ index cards, one for each child in the class, and markers or colored pencils. As you read the poem aloud again, ask children to draw a picture of the wind as a friend in the first stanza, maybe even showing the wind riding piggyback on the biker, using one side of the card. For the second stanza, children can turn the card over and draw what the wind would look like as an enemy. After everyone is finished, display the drawings (some showing the first stanza drawings, some the second stanza drawings) around the poem to show how everyone has a different mental picture from the same poem.

Thursday: Poet's Talk

Patricia Hubbell tells young poets,

"Pay attention to everything. Ask questions, study, look closely, examine. Notice details—is the bird a robin or a thrush? Is the stone quartz or granite? Details make the poem strong."

As you read her poem "When I Ride My Bike," can you see where the poet looked closely and noticed details?

Friday: Craft Talk

◎ **Personification** (or giving human qualities to something that isn't human) is used to bring the wind to life and illustrate how sometimes humans have very personal relationships with elements of the natural world.

◎ This poet writes about an **ordinary experience**—something almost every child can relate to.

◎ **Punctuation: Parentheses** are used in only one place, at the end of the first stanza, to show the action of the wind as if it were an aside, an explanation added on. **Dashes** are used to show the shifts between the narrator and the wind. They also serve to slow the pace in three places. Read the poem aloud and demonstrate how the dashes indicate longer pauses at those points and mark a shift in perspective near the end.

School Bus Lady

I hear the engine rumbling
As she sits out by the street
Waiting for this slowpoke (me)
To climb into his seat.

I don't know how she does it
Every day at 8:03,
But rain or snow or sleet, I know
She's always there for me.

– By J. Patrick Lewis

School Bus Lady

J. Patrick Lewis

Monday: Introduce the Poem (big book page 15)

The Heart of the Poem

Many of you know what it is like to wait for the bus on school mornings. We have seen school buses rolling through streets on the way to school, or city buses on their routes through neighborhoods. Sometimes the bus driver has to wait for us, like the bus driver in this poem has to wait for the slow-poke speaker. We know the buses and the bus drivers come every day, even in bad weather. The speaker in the poem can always count on the bus driver to be there, waiting.

Conversations About the Poem

Just like the speaker in the poem depends on the bus driver to go to school, we all depend on lots of different people to keep our lives running smoothly. Talk to the person next to you about who is always there for you every day, no matter what: it could be your mother, father, or caregiver who meets you after school; it could be a puppy who is always there waiting for you; or even the teacher, me, always here in the classroom waiting for you to arrive.

Tuesday: Ways to Climb Inside the Poem

Choral Reading

Read the poem three times. First, read it to the children to set the tone and pace. Let your voice shift so that the first stanza has more of a sense of rushing—the bus is arriving and you have to hurry. In the second stanza, shift your tone to one of disbelief or wonder. On the second reading, have everyone read together with attention to pacing and tone. On the third reading, divide the class into two groups. Have Group 1 read the first stanza, and have Group 2 read the second stanza. To extend the sound effects and actions from above, have the two groups read the poem again: As Group 1 reads, let Group 2 add sound effects and motions. Then switch on the second stanza.

Acting

Read the poem again. Ask children to add appropriate gestures and sound effects. Try these for a start:

Poem	Actions
I hear the engine rumbling	"Rumble, rumble." (murmur)
As she sits out by the street	Hand poised as if holding the steering wheel.
Waiting for this slowpoke (me)	Glance at your watch and look out the window for
To climb into his seat.	the tardy passenger.

I don't know how she does it
Every day at 8:03,

But rain or snow or sleet, I know
She's always there for me.

Look straight ahead, shrug shoulders.
Show a look of wonder.

Rain—"pitter-patter-pitter-patter." (whisper)
Snow—Hands drift from high to
low, moving fingers.
Sleet—Click fingernails on the tabletop.

Wednesday: Ways to Climb Inside the Poem

Interactive Writing

J. Patrick Lewis chose to focus his poem on the relationship between the speaker and the bus driver—an everyday person with whom the speaker shares a connection. Make a list together of people your students see every day (or many days)—for example, school aides or cafeteria workers, custodians, police officers or firefighters, and people who work in local shops. Choose one individual to write about, and title your poem with the person's job. Then have the children list ways to describe this person. You may want to give a copy of the poem to the person, or invite the individual into your classroom to hear the children read the poem.

Thursday: Poet's Talk

J. Patrick Lewis says,

> "If you want to do a favor for a child who tells you he wants to be a writer, hand him a dictionary."

I think that's very interesting advice. Why would you hand a child a dictionary if he or she wants to be writer? Does anybody have any ideas about this?

Friday: Craft Talk

- ❂ The poet uses **sound words**, or **onomatopoeia** (*rumbling*). Poets use all of their senses when describing the world of a poem. Adding sound words is a simple way to help children practice using their sense of hearing in their writing.

- ❂ This poem might be considered to be an **ode** to the bus driver. An ode is a poem celebrating or praising someone or something. Children may be encouraged to write odes to people or things in their own lives.

Poem for My Friend

A star
Is like the sun
Only far away.
When you
Are far away
You
Are like a star
And I think about your twinkle.

When you are near
You are the sun—
I feel your warmth.

– By Patricia Hubbell

Poem for My Friend

Patricia Hubbell

Monday: Introduce the Poem (big book page 16)

The Heart of the Poem

There is something in this poem that poets do all the time when they write—they compare things (which means they say something is like something else). In this poem, a friend is compared to a star and the sun. When the friend is far away, he or she is like a star, and when the friend is close, he or she is like the sun. Listen and see if you know what the poet is trying to share about a friend.

Conversations About the Poem

Can you think of a time when one of your friends was far away and felt like a distant star? And can you think of how you felt when your friend was near again—did it feel warm like the sun? Share your thoughts with the person next to you.

Tuesday: Ways to Climb Inside the Poem

Choral Reading

This poem compares the feelings of being near a friend and being far away from a friend. This poem invites two voices, so divide the class into two groups to read the two perspectives.

Poem	*Readers*
A star	Groups 1 and 2
Is like the sun	
Only far away.	
When you	Group 1
Are far away	
You	
Are like a star	
And I think about your twinkle.	
When you are near	Group 2
You are the sun—	
I feel your warmth.	

Wednesday: Ways to Climb Inside the Poem

Illustrating

The poem holds so much sweetness and affection for the speaker's friend—something that all children can relate to. Have each child think of a beloved friend or relative and draw a picture of him or her. Children who are writing independently can write their own friendship poems to go along with the portrait—encourage them to use comparisons to describe their friend or their friendship, as the poet did. If your students are not yet writing independently, you can ask them to tell you what they might compare their friend to, and then write it for them at the bottom of their pictures.

Thursday: Poet's Talk

Listen to what the poet Patricia Hubbell says about poetry:

"Poetry writing helps you to share your feelings and to make yourself known in a new way."

A lot of poets feel this way about writing poems. As we reread Patricia Hubbell's poem, "Poem for My Friend," do you think she shares her feelings and makes herself known in a new way?

Friday: Craft Talk

- ◎ The poet uses a **simile** (you may choose to use the word "comparison" when talking to your students about this) when she describes her friend as being "*like* a star" when she is far away. The word *like* shows that the poet is using a simile.

- ◎ The poet uses **line breaks** and **white space** to slow the reader down and emphasize certain parts of the poem. For example, in the middle of the poem, the word *You* (referring to the speaker's friend) is set apart on its own line, perhaps because the "you" is the most important part of the poem.

- ◎ **Punctuation:** The poet uses a **dash** after *sun*, instead of a comma, which makes the pause after the line a little longer.

Best Friend

I've got a pixie, you've got a braid.
   I love the sunshine, you like the shade.
I'll find a frog by the side of the road.
   You'll spot a cloud that is shaped like a toad.
You'll paint a picture, I'll climb a tree.
   You will be you and I will be me.
Strawberry, rhubarb, somehow we blend,
   We are each other's very best friend.

   – By Marilyn Singer

Best Friend
Marilyn Singer

Monday: Introduce the Poem (big book page 17)

The Heart of the Poem
You usually expect that best friends are the same—they like to play the same things—they might even dress the same way—but in the poem "Best Friend" listen to all the ways that the best friends are different.

Conversations About the Poem
What are some of the ways that the best friends in the poem are different? Now think about your best friend. Turn and share with the person next to you ways that your best friend is different from you. Now that you've talked with your neighbor, let's share a few ideas as a group. How do your differences make your friendship stronger or more interesting?

Tuesday: Ways to Climb Inside the Poem

Choral Reading
This poem is excellent for choral reading because it can be read as the friends' two voices talking in alternate lines.

Divide the class into two groups. Assign the first group the voice of the first friend (lines 1, 3, 5), and the second group the voice of the second friend (lines 2, 4, 6). Point out that some lines can have both voices speaking. Ask the two groups to say the last two lines together, and the title.

Using a pointer, point to the words of the poem for a choral reading.

Wednesday: Ways to Climb Inside the Poem

Illustrating
Ask your students to think of someone they are close to, who is very different from them. Have them fold a regular-sized piece of blank paper in half. On one side, have them draw a picture of themselves, and on the other side, a picture of their friend or loved one. Children who are just beginning to write conventionally may be able to write words next to each drawing that relate to things that person likes. Children

who are more experienced writers will be able to write a list of sentences describing what each person likes or likes to do. You may want to have your students share in pairs, discussing the things about themselves and their loved ones that are similar and the things that are different.

Another take on visually representing this poem might be to make a Venn diagram of the self and the friend in the poem. Have children write or draw things that are distinct about each friend in the side sections, and note things that are the same in the overlapping section.

Thursday: Poet's Talk

Marilyn Singer writes that as a poet, she spends

". . . a lot of time looking and listening, both to the natural world and to the urban landscape. I pay attention to people and their conversations, too."

I wonder if she got any of her ideas for "Best Friend" by looking, listening, and paying attention to people. What details or ideas in "Best Friend" might have come from doing those things?

Friday: Craft Talk

◎ The poet uses **opposites**, or **contrasts**, to more fully describe the relationship of the two friends in the poem. Many poems include contrasting perspectives.

◎ The poet uses the **metaphor** (you may choose to use the word "comparison" when talking to your students about this) of strawberry and rhubarb to describe the friends' relationship—strawberry and rhubarb are very different, but they combine to make a delicious pie, just as the two very different friends have a wonderful friendship together.

◎ The poet uses **specific description** when telling us what the two friends like. This not only creates genuine characters, but it also helps us see the world of the poem very clearly.

◎ The poem is written in **rhyming couplets** (two rhyming lines) which are kind of like the two best friends in the poem—different yet the same (*braid/shade*; *road/toad*; *tree/me*; *blend/friend*).

Birthday Candles

Today
I am the star
of birthdays!
Of ice cream,
of cake,
of candles.
I get one secret wish,
(here comes my favorite part . . .)
  whoossshhhhh, whew!
Those candle flames go out,
but the wish stays in
my heart.

— By Rebecca Kai Dotlich

Birthday Candles
Rebecca Kai Dotlich

Monday: Introduce the Poem (big book page 18)

The Heart of the Poem

Sometimes poets choose to describe just one small (but important) moment of an experience, as Rebecca Kai Dotlich does in her poem "Birthday Candles." Listen to how she slows down and tells us every detail about the moment of blowing out birthday candles and making a wish.

Conversations About the Poem

Many people can relate to the experience of blowing out birthday candles—I know that some of you start counting down the days until your birthdays when they are still months away! Right now, close your eyes and think back to a birthday that you remember really clearly—try to zoom in on the time when the candles were lit and it was time for you to make a wish. Can you see yourself making a wish? Do you remember your wish? Has your wish stayed in your heart like the wish stayed in this poet's heart? Did you keep your wish a secret, or did you share it with someone else? When you tell the person next to you about this special moment, see if you can really slow down and tell everything that happened.

Tuesday: Ways to Climb Inside the Poem

Illustrating

This poem is not about an entire birthday party; it zooms in on one small moment of a whole birthday—the time when the candles are lit and it's time to make a wish. Ask students to think about their last birthday party and see it as a movie in their minds. Guide them with questions about what they see, who is there, what foods they are eating, and so on. Try to zoom in on one small moment. Have them practice retelling that moment, taking care to really slow down and say everything that happened. Then ask them to draw a picture of that moment, including all of the details they mentioned in their retelling. If your students are writing independently, you may choose to have them write their own birthday poems and wishes to go along with their pictures.

Wednesday: Ways to Climb Inside the Poem

Celebrating Special Occasions

Bring in or make a picture of a birthday cake to display on the wall, and display the poem "Birthday Candles" next to the cake. Tell students that the class may want to read this poem aloud to a birthday girl or boy in the class. Make small drawings of candles, and each time it's a child's birthday, ask the birthday child to draw a picture of a wish or write a wish on a candle and attach it to the picture of the cake.

Thursday: Poet's Talk

The poet Rebecca Kai Dotlich says,

"Poetry matters because it holds the key. The key to our heart, to our inner voice, to our soul."

As I read her poem "Birthday Candles" to you again, let's listen to see where her idea about poetry holding the key to our hearts is reflected in her poem.

Friday: Craft Talk

- The use of **line breaks** and **white space** suggests how the poem should be paced as it is read aloud.

- The use of **sound words** (*whoossshhhhh, whew!*) clearly illustrates the moment of blowing out candles. Adding sound is a simple way for children to make their poems more detailed and to practice using their senses in their poems.

- The poem has a tight **focus** on one small part of the birthday celebration. Because poetry is very condensed writing, focusing on one small moment is particularly important.

- **Punctuation:** The poet uses **exclamation marks** for emphasis. She also uses a **parenthesis** as an aside to the reader and then an **ellipsis** to extend the waiting until the next line.

Song for My Swing

Swing, swing,
Float me high
Into the blue, bird fluttering sky,
Tip my feet down low to grass
Where ants and caterpillars pass
Fling me loose once more through air
Till I skim the grass with my rippling hair.
Lift me, swing, high into space—
Fly my heart to a brand-new place.

– By Patricia Hubbell

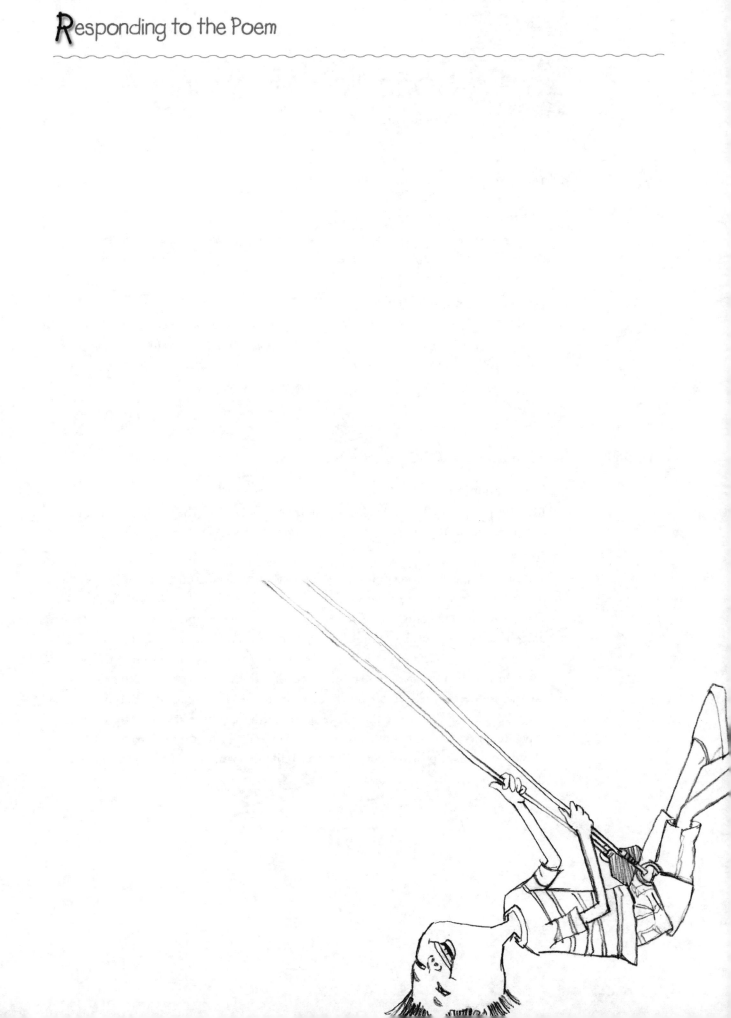

Song for My Swing

Patricia Hubbell

Monday: Introduce the Poem (big book page 19)

The Heart of the Poem

Can you remember a time when you were swinging on the swings and you felt as if you were flying in the air? In this poem, the poet talks to a swing! As she speaks to the swing, she describes exactly what she loves about swinging.

Conversations About the Poem

Put your thumbs up if you have floated through the air on a swing like this. What are some words that the poet, Patricia Hubbell, uses to describe exactly what swinging high is like? Turn and share with a neighbor what you can remember from the poem. When you've done that, see if you can think of some ways to describe exactly how you feel when you are swinging.

Tuesday: Ways to Climb Inside the Poem

Choral Reading

Read the poem once through again to establish a cadence and pace. Then have the class read the poem in unison, swaying forward and backward as you read.

Illustrating

Tell the children that you would like them to think like illustrators as you reread the poem, and to pay special attention to the way the poem describes what it's like to swing way up high. For example, in line 3, instead of saying "into the sky," the poet describes it as "the blue, bird fluttering sky." This gives us a picture in our minds. Ask the children to pay attention to the pictures in their minds as they listen to the poem again. Invite them to share these mind-pictures with the person next to them. Next, ask the children to each choose one line or part of the poem to illustrate. You may choose to have them rewrite the line or lines they have chosen at the bottom of their paper, or you can copy, cut out, and paste the lines to the bottom of a paper. These illustrations can be posted sequentially on a bulletin board or in the hallway, next to the poem.

Wednesday: Ways to Climb Inside the Poem

Interactive Writing

In "Song for My Swing," the poet chose to address her poem to the swing itself. Together as a class, brainstorm a list of other playground equipment—slides, monkey bars, and so on. Choose one, and write the title "Song for My _____" at the top of a sheet of chart paper. Have your students close their eyes and imagine what it feels like to play on that piece of equipment. Collect their ideas into a poem. Before doing this project, you may want to take the children on a short "research trip" to a playground.

Thursday: Poet's Talk

The poet Patricia Hubbell says a very interesting thing about how she gets ideas for her poems:

"Looking for poem subjects is a bit like going fishing—you wait for the tug on the line and then you reel in your catch—not a fish, but a poem!"

"Waiting for the tug on the line" . . . What does she mean? Has anyone here ever felt that way about writing? Maybe we should think about that when we write!

Friday: Craft Talk

◉ The poet uses **white space** and **line breaks** to visually mimic the motion of a swing. The lines look like a swing moving out and coming back. Encourage students to think about how their poems look and how that affects the way they are read.

◉ This poem is addressed to an everyday object. When poets address their poem to an object or person, it's called an **apostrophe poem**. It can be interesting for children to shift the perspective in their writing and write *to* the thing or person they are describing, instead of just writing *about* it.

◉ This poem uses a **metaphor** (or comparison) in the last line. The speaker's heart is not really going to be flying to a brand-new place. You can ask students what the metaphor in the poem means.

◉ This poem uses many strong verbs to describe the action of the poem. Ask your students to point to a few of these strong, **vivid verbs** (or action words).

◉ **Punctuation:** Notice how the poet **capitalizes** the first letter of every line. The **dash** marks the shift from the specific description of swinging to the metaphor in the last line.

The Stray Dog

I wonder what he finds to eat
in smelly garbage heaps.
When the night is cold like this
I wonder where he sleeps.
I wonder why he crouches down
and trembles while he's chewing.
Do people shout and chase him
when they see what he is doing?
This morning when he snatched the half
of sandwich that I threw
I know I saw him give his stumpy tail
a wag or two.
I wonder if he might begin
to trust someone who's kind.
I wonder, when she sees he's thin,
if Mom might change her mind.

— By Alice Schertle

The Stray Dog
Alice Schertle

Monday: Introduce the Poem (big book page 20)

The Heart of the Poem

In this poem by Alice Schertle, the speaker is wondering about a stray dog she or he knows. She repeats the words "I wonder" several times. The speaker's wonderings give us a clear picture of what the stray dog's life is like. As you listen to the poem, think about what the speaker in the poem is wondering about the stray dog.

Conversations About the Poem

What does the speaker in this poem wonder about the stray dog? Turn to the person next to you and share what you remember. Has anybody ever seen a stray dog on the street or in your neighborhood? What are some things you remember about the dog?

Tuesday: Ways to Climb Inside the Poem

Acting and Choral Reading

Divide the class into two groups. Group 1 will repeat the words "I wonder" as you point to those words in the poem, and Group 2 will act out the actions of the stray dog. You can read the rest of the line after "I wonder . . ." as Group 2 acts out the actions of the dog. For example, in lines 1 and 2, the first group will say the words "I wonder," and while you read the rest of the lines, the second group will be acting out the actions of the dog. You might talk about ways that they can act out the last two lines using hand movements or other actions.

Wednesday: Ways to Climb Inside the Poem

Shared Writing

This poem might be called a list poem because it is essentially a list of the poet's won-derings about a stray dog. List poems provide a wonderful structure for shared writing experiences. Using the repeating phrase "I wonder," write your own list poem as a class. To save time, you may want to choose a topic that all students will be able to relate to (for example, a tree in the school's playground, a fire truck seen on a recent class trip to the firehouse, or something that relates to your particular curriculum). Using the repeating phrase "I wonder," build a poem together.

Thursday: Poet's Talk

The poet Alice Schertle says that she gets ideas for poems from

"images, sounds, feelings . . . a traffic jam, the taste of pizza, sand in my shoe. . . ."
The best inspiration of all, I think, is an SSN, a Sudden Strange Notion."

A notion is a thought or an idea, and Alice Schertle calls it an SSN, a Sudden Strange Notion. I'm thinking of this idea about an SSN and her poem "The Stray Dog," and I'm wondering if maybe she saw a stray dog on a street and got an SSN and decided to write a poem. Has anyone here ever gotten an SSN to write something?

Friday: Craft Talk

- This poem is essentially a **list poem**—a simple, kid-friendly form that in this case uses the repeating phrase "I wonder." List poems can be built around various repeating phrases—"I like . . . ," "I wish . . . ," and so on. Even very beginning writers often feel successful when encouraged to use this simple structure.

- The **repetition** of the phrase "I wonder" builds on the rhythm of the poem. Repeating a line or a phrase helps children discover how to create rhythm in their own poetry.

Puppy Love

Oh, puppy love,
Oh, dog divine,
I really wish
That you were mine.

I see you in
The window, framed,
And all at once
I have you named.

But I'm allergic,
So you see
You never can
Belong to me.

       – By Jane Yolen

Puppy Love
Jane Yolen

Monday: Introduce the Poem (big book page 21)

The Heart of the Poem

The poem "Puppy Love" is about how the speaker of the poem really wants a puppy he or she sees in the window of a pet store. The poet, Jane Yolen, surprises us at the end of the poem from what we might have expected when we started reading. Listen as I read, and we'll talk about the surprise ending when I'm finished.

Conversations About the Poem

Were you surprised by the ending of the poem? What surprised you? Turn and tell the person next to you.

Tuesday: Ways to Climb Inside the Poem

Acting

This poem is presented in three parts or **stanzas**. Each stanza can be acted out. In the first stanza, one group of children could be portraying the longing and desire for the puppy. How would they show with their hands how much they really want a puppy? In the second stanza, the next group can act out peering through the window and could whisper a puppy's name. The final group could begin blinking their eyes and rubbing their noses while the stanza is being read. The finale could be one big sneeze from the whole class.

Wednesday: Ways to Climb Inside the Poem

Illustrating

Ask the children if they have ever experienced the feeling of wanting something very badly and not being able to have it, just as the child in the poem longs for a puppy that he or she is allergic to. Have your students draw and write (as they are able) about the thing they want but cannot have. If your students are writing independently, have them write *to* the thing they are describing instead of just writing *about* it—just as Jane Yolen does in her poem about the puppy.

Thursday: Poet's Talk

Jane Yolen says that for her,

"Poetry is emotion made . . . real. It reminds us of who we are, what we feel."

As I read what Jane Yolen says about poetry, I'm reminded of her poem "Puppy Love." It's one of those poems that tells the truth about how the speaker feels. Let me read the poem again, and after I finish, turn to someone next to you and discuss how this poem "reminds us of who we are, and what we feel."

Friday: Craft Talk

- **Rhyme**—in this poem, lines 1 and 3 do not rhyme but lines 2 and 4 do. Notice how this pattern keeps the flow of the poem from becoming too "singsongy." More sophisticated young writers will be able to notice and discuss this.

- The speaker in the poem speaks directly *to* the puppy. This kind of a poem, in which the speaker addresses an object or person, is called an **apostrophe poem**. Shifting the perspective from writing about something to writing to something can be an interesting device for children to try out in their own poems.

Just Like Grandpa

I sneak into his closet,
put on Grandpa's hat,
pull it down like Grandpa does
and give the top a pat.
I slip into his jacket,
which hangs below my knees,
then slide my feet inside his shoes . . .
and Grandpa never sees
I'm standing on my tiptoes
as tall as I can get.
He always shakes my hand and says
"I don't believe we've met."

       — By Alice Schertle

Just Like Grandpa

Alice Schertle

Monday: Introduce the Poem (big book page 22)

The Heart of the Poem

Have you ever played "dress-up," or put on the clothes of someone else and played a pretend game? In this poem, the speaker actually steps inside Grandpa's clothes to see how it feels! The poet uses clear verbs (or action words) to describe exactly what the speaker is doing while dressing up like Grandpa.

Conversations About the Poem

It was easy to see in our minds exactly what the speaker was doing when dressing up like Grandpa because the poet used such clear verbs (or action words). Let's try to remember together what exactly the speaker did. Turn and tell someone next to you what you remember. Now let's make a list together on the board of the verbs in the poem.

Tuesday: Ways to Climb Inside the Poem

Dressing Up and Writing

If your classroom has a dress-up or costume center, you may choose to work with a small group of children during center time to make poems about the people they become when they dress up. If your students are not yet writing independently, ask them to describe who they become when they are wearing, for example, the fairy wings or the magician's cape or the police hat. If your students are writing independently, they may want to write a poem about pretending to be someone else. You can read these little poems to the class when choice time is over, and then post them in your pretend area.

Wednesday: Ways to Climb Inside the Poem

Acting

Stretch the idea of choral reading just a bit with this one. Read the lines together, and add a gesture for each action. For example:

Poem	Actions
I sneak into his closet,	Crouch down and step in place as if sneaking in.
put on Grandpa's hat,	Reach up as if placing a hat on your head.

Since the actions are so explicit, this one will be easy for the children to catch on to.

Interactive Writing

The strong verbs in this poem are responsible for its clarity. For a wonderful exercise in thinking of specific verbs as opposed to general ones, you can have one child pantomime an everyday task in front of the class, and list together specifically what that child is doing. You can encourage children to become more and more specific with their descriptions. For example, if a child is pantomiming brushing her teeth, your students will probably first say, "brushing her teeth." You can encourage them to describe exactly what the child is doing with her body: "lifting her arm, scrubbing up and down, turning her head from side to side," and so on.

Thursday: Poet's Talk

Alice Schertle says,

"Poetry speaks to the heart and to the mind. A cherished poem is a gift that we may carry with us all our lives."

Does anybody know what Alice Schertle means with these words? Is there a poem that you've heard or read that you carry around with you? We'll come back to this quote often. We can even display it on the wall or near the poetry books.

Friday: Craft Talk

◎ The poet uses **specific verbs** to clarify what the speaker is doing while dressing up like Grandpa. Encouraging children to use specific verbs will strengthen the description in their poems as well.

◎ The **rhythm** of this poem makes it easy to read in phrases. Each line becomes a phrase unit. Try reading it aloud with that in mind.

Happy Teeth

I put a tooth under my pillow
And got a quarter. I was four.

And now I'm five. I put two teeth
Under my pillow. I got more.

If I keep losing teeth like this,
The Tooth Fairy will come again,

And when she stops I won't complain
'Cause I'll be rich when I am ten.

— By J. Patrick Lewis

Happy Teeth

J. Patrick Lewis

Monday: Introduce the Poem (big book page 23)

The Heart of the Poem

Several of you have a missing-tooth smile, just like the speaker in this poem! In "Happy Teeth," the speaker describes something most of you can relate to—putting lost teeth under a pillow and discovering what the tooth fairy has left. In the last two lines, the poem makes us laugh. Why? Listen!

Conversations About the Poem

What was funny in this poem? What happens at your house when someone loses a tooth? Turn and tell the person next to you.

Tuesday: Ways to Climb Inside the Poem

Illustrating

One of the wonderful things about the tooth fairy mentioned in J. Patrick Lewis's poem is that everyone gets to imagine their own version of what the tooth fairy looks like. Have the children draw a picture of the tooth fairy.

Wednesday: Ways to Climb Inside the Poem

Choral Reading

After you have read this to your class two or three times, divide the children into two groups. Group 1 reads the first line of each stanza, and Group 2 reads the second line of each stanza. Everyone reads the final stanza together as one collective voice.

Acting

Follow the lines of the poem and count how much money the speaker of the poem will have by the last line. Bring in a pillow and some quarters, and ask students to pretend they are the tooth fairy and for each year place a quarter or quarters under the pillow. How much money will the speaker have by age ten? Will the speaker be rich?

Thursday: Poet's Talk

Poet J. Patrick Lewis says,

"Poetry gives the reader the 'ah-ha' experience, by which he or she will look at something now in a way he or she had never thought to do before."

What part of this poem "Happy Teeth" helped you "look at something in a new way?" Turn and tell someone next to you.

Friday: Craft Talk

◎ The poet uses a **rhyme scheme** where lines 2 and 4 rhyme as do lines 6 and 8. However, lines 1, 3, 5, and 7 do not rhyme. As you read this poem aloud, notice how the rhyming words are the words on which you pause. More sophisticated young writers will be able to notice and discuss this pattern.

◎ The speaker exaggerates in the last line, " 'Cause I'll be rich when I am ten." This kind of exaggeration is called **hyperbole**. It's a big word, but kids love to repeat it out loud.

The Cedar Tree

When I was only six years old
My grampa went with me
Into the woods where we could
find a little cedar tree.

And though it was so tiny
I held it in one hand
He said that one day it would be
bigger than any man.

We planted it in our back yard
below the old stone wall.
I watered it and watched it,
but it didn't grow at all.

It seemed to me that it just stayed
that same small size forever.
If you'd asked me then "When will it grow?"
I would have answered "Never."

Then I forgot about it
for two years or maybe three
until one day I realized
it was twice as tall as me.

That day I learned a lesson.
Although it might seem slow
sometimes, just like that cedar tree,
good things take time to grow.

     – By Joseph Bruchac

The Cedar Tree

Joseph Bruchac

Monday: Introduce the Poem (big book pages 24 and 25)

The Heart of the Poem

Sometimes poems can be used to teach a lesson or tell us about something the poet or speaker has learned. In this poem, a grandfather and grandchild plant a tree together. As the tree grows, the child learns an important life lesson. As I read the poem, think about what the grandfather taught the child.

Conversations About the Poem

Do any of you remember something you wanted to have very quickly, but it took a long time? Was it hard to wait? Was it worth waiting for? Now share your thinking with the person next to you.

Tuesday: Ways to Climb Inside the Poem

Choral Reading and Acting

Divide the class into three groups. Group 1 reads the first and fourth stanzas. Group 2 reads the second and fifth stanzas. Group 3 reads the third and sixth stanzas.

If the children aren't yet ready to read, have the groups act out their stanzas while you read them aloud.

Wednesday: Ways to Climb Inside the Poem

Illustrating

Reread the poem aloud, and remind the students of your conversation about what the child learned about patience from the grandfather and the cedar tree. Make a "before and after" picture of your own to use as a model. In the "before" picture, you might show the child holding the tiny cedar tree in one hand. In the "after" picture, you might show the child standing next to a cedar tree that has grown twice as tall as the child. Now invite the children to reflect on the thing in their own lives that they wanted to happen quickly but didn't. Provide materials for them to make a "before and after" picture to show the changes that occurred as they waited.

Alternatively, you may divide the class into six small groups and assign each group one stanza of the poem to illustrate. You can post the pictures sequentially, with each stanza written out below.

Thursday: Poet's Talk

The poet, Joseph Bruchac, tells us,

"What inspires me to write a poem? It is this business of living, life itself."

Turn to someone next to you and talk about how you see this idea reflected in his poem, "The Cedar Tree."

Friday: Craft Talk

- The poet uses a **rhyme scheme** in which lines 2 and 4 rhyme in each stanza. As you read this aloud, notice how the rhyming words are the words on which you pause. More sophisticated young writers will be able to notice and discuss this pattern.

- The poet tells a story with his verses; this is called a **narrative poem**. Each stanza moves you through the story sequentially, almost like turning the pages in a picture book. This poem provides a good jumping-off point for a discussion about how some poems tell a story and some don't.

Laundromat

When Mom goes to the laundromat
I come along. I'm old
Enough to carry stacks of stuff
And I know how to fold.

We shell out quarters. Underwear
Swirls in a soapy waltz,
Socks leapfrog over other socks,
Pop's pants do somersaults.

We drag 'em out. The dryer drum
Starts overturning. See
My bathrobe rock-and-rolling round—
More action than TV!

And when at last we're driving home
I dream beside a pile
Of fresh clean clothes and toast my face.
Hey, that's my favorite mile.

                    — By X. J. Kennedy

Laundromat

X. J. Kennedy

Monday: Introduce the Poem (big book pages 26 and 27)

The Heart of the Poem

Often writers find poetry in ordinary, everyday events—even in chores as boring as doing the laundry! The family in this poem does their laundry at a laundromat. The speaker watches the clothes tumbling around inside the machines and describes what happens in some really unusual ways.

Conversations About the Poem

Instead of just telling us that the clothes go around in circles in the dryer, the poet makes laundry exciting by seeing it and writing about it in an unusual way. How did the speaker in the poem describe the way the family's clothes twirl and spin around? Let's share some of the parts you remember. Now take a moment to think about some of the chores you help out with at home. Do you think that you could find poetry in a chore the way this poet did?

Tuesday: Ways to Climb Inside the Poem

Acting

Ask your students to think about how the poet chose words that make the laundry move around in our minds. Highlight *somersault*, *leapfrog*, *waltz*, and so on. Next, divide the class into halves. One group will be readers, and the other group will be actors. As the poem is being read, actors can act out the action. The italicized words from the excerpts listed below can be given a specific motion or gesture to bring another dimension to the poem.

- I'm old / Enough to *carry* stacks of stuff / And I know how to *fold*.

- We *shell out* quarters. Underwear / *Swirls* in a soapy waltz, / Socks *leapfrog* over other socks, / Pop's pants do *somersaults*.

- We *drag* 'em out. The dryer drum / Starts *overturning*. See / My bathrobe *rock-and-rolling* round—

- And when at last we're *driving* home / I *dream* beside a pile / Of fresh clean clothes and *toast* my face.

After one performance, have the two groups switch roles.

Wednesday: Ways to Climb Inside the Poem

Interactive Writing

Make a list together of the household chores your students participate in at home. Choose one of these chores, and talk about ways that students could envision that chore in a brand-new way. Remind them how the speaker in "Laundromat" sees, instead of a mess of clothes in the dryer, "socks leapfrog over other socks" and a bathrobe "rock-and-rolling round." Write the chore you've chosen at the top of a piece of chart paper. Now list your students' ideas about how they can make that chore more interesting by seeing it in brand-new, unusual ways—just as X. J. Kennedy did in "Laundromat."

Thursday: Poet's Talk

X. J. Kennedy writes,

> "[Some poems] begin when I notice something, or experience something . . . that, for reasons I don't always understand, sets off strong feelings."

When we reread his poem "Laundromat," we feel that we're almost there in the laundromat and that we can see what the speaker sees. Which part of the poem shows that this experience "sets off strong feelings" for the speaker?

Friday: Craft Talk

- The poet uses a specific **rhyme pattern** within each stanza: lines 1 and 3 do not rhyme: lines 2 and 4 do rhyme. More sophisticated young writers may be able to examine and try out rhyme schemes in their own poems.

- The poet uses **metaphor** to describe the way the laundry moves, comparing it to dancing and playing. Unexpected **images** are created in the readers' minds. Children may be encouraged to describe ordinary events in unusual ways, as the poet does in this poem: "underwear swirls in a soapy waltz," "socks leapfrog," "pants do somersaults," "bathrobe rock-and-rolling."

- The poet uses **specific verbs** to clarify exactly what is happening as the family does laundry (*carry, fold, shell out, waltz, leapfrog, somersault, drag, toast*). Encouraging children to use specific verbs will strengthen the description in their poems as well.

Emma

Emma knows one thing for sure:
there are too many choices.

Too much to do.

So many voices inside her head.

Quiet. Shy.
Shouting. Loud.
Asking. Telling. Begging. Tired.

There's so much

listening

required.

> — By Janet Wong

Emma

Janet Wong

Monday: Introduce the Poem (big book page 28)

The Heart of the Poem

Sometimes poets help us get inside other people's thoughts, as poet Janet Wong does in this poem about a little girl named Emma. Emma thinks that it is really hard to have to listen to all of the different voices in her own head!

Conversations About the Poem

Think about all of the different voices in Emma's head. Let's list out what you remember about them. Just like Emma, all humans are complicated mixes of feelings—that's part of what makes being a person so interesting! Do you ever feel like you have lots of different voices or feelings inside you, and that they don't always agree with each other or with what's going on outside of you?

Tuesday: Ways to Climb Inside the Poem

Illustrating

Invite kids to think about all the different voices and feelings they might have inside their heads. Then ask your students to draw self-portraits of just their faces, having them write words inside the self-portrait that describe the different "voices" they hear or thoughts and feelings they have. You may want to have them brainstorm a list of ideas before beginning.

Wednesday: Ways to Climb Inside the Poem

Choral Reading

This poem lends itself to a playful reading. Since Emma is listening to so many voices in her head, you and your class can have fun with this one—this may be a louder choral reading than most, to mimic the confusion in Emma's mind. You may decide to whisper the words "Quiet" and "Shy." Shout the words "Shouting" and "Loud," and so on. Here is an example of how the poem might be read chorally:

Poem	Readers
Emma knows one thing for sure:	[all voices]
there are too many choices.	[half the class]
Too much to do.	[half the class]
So many voices inside her head.	[all voices]
Quiet. Shy.	[Divide the class into 8 groups and have
Shouting. Loud.	each group read one of the 8 voice words.]
Asking. Telling. Begging. Tired.	
There's so much	[all voices]
listening	[half the class]
required.	[half the class]

Thursday: Poet's Talk

Janet Wong, the poet who wrote "Emma," says,

"Most of my poems start with ideas: thinking about childhood memories."

Even though Janet Wong's name isn't Emma, I can see where the poet might have remembered the feeling of being a child like Emma and having so many voices in her head. Have you ever felt the way Emma feels in this poem? Turn to the person next to you and share.

Friday: Craft Talk

- ◎ The poet uses **line breaks** and **white space** to let us know when to speed up and when to slow down as we read. While this is difficult for many children to replicate in their own poems, many will be able to notice and discuss how white space and line breaks affect the reading of other people's poems.

- ◎ The poet uses a **list** to describe Emma's conflicting voices or feelings. Listing is a simple technique that will help many young poets add detail to their own poems.

Spring Riddles

Frogs lay eggs,
Tadpoles hatch—
A thousand riddles
In the batch

All heads and tails
They are, and gills,
No feet or other
Froggy frills

(Unlike a snake
Whose eggs will hatch
And—presto!—get
A perfect match.)

Why do frogs take
This odd detour
To get to where
They're heading for?

— By Beverly McLoughland

Spring Riddles
Beverly McLoughland

Monday: Introduce the Poem (big book page 29)

The Heart of the Poem

Can anyone say what a riddle is? It's kind of like a word puzzle; it usually has a question that we have to think about to answer. Sometimes a riddle poem has a clear answer, and sometimes it doesn't—like in "Spring Riddles" by Beverly McLoughland. The poet asks us to think about frogs as they grow. The riddle is: Why do tadpoles (baby frogs) look so different from grown frogs? Think about other animal babies: a kitten looks just like a cat but much smaller; a puppy looks like a small dog; a baby bird is just a small bird; and, as the poem mentions, a baby snake looks exactly like a big snake but smaller. Now, think about a baby frog (a tadpole). Has anyone ever seen a tadpole? It has no legs, a big head, and a tail; it doesn't look anything like a grown-up frog. Strange! The poem is a riddle that may never be solved!

Conversations About the Poem

There are lots of mysteries in nature. The growth of frogs is definitely one of them. Does anyone have a theory of why baby frogs or tadpoles look the way they do? Turn to the person next to you and give an answer.

How does the poet describe the "detour" that frogs take as they grow? What images do you remember? Turn and tell the person next to you.

Tuesday: Ways to Climb Inside the Poem

Choral Reading

The poem is laid out in four stanzas. Read the poem twice. The first time through, have everyone read together. For the second reading, divide the class into two groups. Have Group 1 read stanzas 1 and 3, while Group 2 responds with stanzas 2 and 4.

Interactive Writing

Nature is full of mysteries that we can explore in poems. The transformation of tadpoles into frogs is one of them. List together some of the "mysteries" in nature that your students are curious about. Younger children may need more support with this brainstorming project. For example, you might suggest the transformation of caterpillars into butterflies as an example, or prompt the children to think about other things that they wonder about in the natural world. Lightning, thunder, earthquakes, and so on would all make interesting subjects for riddle poems. Choose one, and then have your students describe what they wonder about it.

Wednesday: Ways to Climb Inside the Poem

Content Exploration

This is a perfect poem to inspire a link to nonfiction, and a discussion about ways in which poets use facts in poems. Read the poem aloud line-by-line and ask children to try and identify which lines contain a fact. For example, you may ask them if the first line, "Frogs lay eggs," is a fact. Highlight or list all the facts and information that the class has learned from this one poem. Bring in a nonfiction book about tadpoles to extend children's interest in tadpoles and frogs.

Thursday: Poet's Talk

Beverly McLoughland writes,

"Many [poems] come from my sense of wonder and curiosity about animals and the natural world. The two poems in this book began that way. 'Spring Riddles' came from my amazement at how strangely nature works sometimes—that from a frog's eggs come these funny-looking tadpole-y creatures—instead of frogs!"

We can feel the poet's wonder and curiosity coming from the words of the poem as we read. Let's read the poem again to remind us how wonder and curiosity can spark a poem.

Friday: Craft Talk

- ◎ The poet uses a **rhyme scheme** in which lines 2 and 4 rhyme, as do lines 6 and 8. However lines 1, 3, 5, and 7 do not. As you read this aloud, notice how the rhyming words are the words on which you pause. More sophisticated young readers will be able to notice and discuss the pattern.

- ◎ This poem is a **riddle**. Children will love collecting and discussing other examples of riddle poems. (See the bibliography in the *Reading and Writing About Poetry Across the Year* guidebook for riddle poem collections by Rebecca Kai Dotlich, Douglas Florian, Nikki Grimes, and Jack Prelutsky.)

- ◎ **Punctuation:** The poet uses **parentheses** to give the reader a fact about another animal—the snake.

Sun and Moon: A Poem for Two Voices

I'm the sun.
I make the day.
Earth turns toward me.
Night fades away.

> I'm the Moon,
> and since my birth
> each month I loop
> around the Earth.

I'm quite different
than you are.
I'm heat and light.
I am a star.

I'm the Moon,
Earth's satellite
Dark and cold,
I'm only bright
When I reflect
your distant light.

I light the day.

I charm the night.

– By Bobbi Katz

Sun and Moon:
A Poem for Two Voices
Bobbi Katz

Monday: Introduce the Poem (big book pages 30 and 31)

The Heart of the Poem
Sometimes poets imagine the voices of things that can't really talk to us, as Bobbi Katz does in her poem about the moon and the sun. Listen carefully as I read—you'll hear two different voices. One voice is the voice of the sun, and one is the voice of the moon. The poem is like a conversation between the two.

Conversations About the Poem
We get a very strong sense of the different personalities of the moon and the sun by listening to this pretend conversation between them. What did you hear the sun and the moon saying to each other? Turn and tell the person next to you.

Tuesday: Ways to Climb Inside the Poem

Choral Reading
Read through the poem once to set a pace and model intonation. Be sure to model a difference between the voices of the sun and the moon. Divide your class into two groups. Have one group read the voice of the sun and ask the other group to respond with the voice of the moon.

Interactive Writing
Ask the children to think about other things in nature that might have a conversation if they could (for example, bees and flowers, birds and trees, night and day). Then choose a pair, and list ideas together to write your own poem for two voices. (See "Poems for Two Voices" in "Part Three: Writing Poetry" in the *Reading and Writing Poetry Across the Year* guidebook.)

Wednesday: Ways to Climb Inside the Poem

Content Exploration

This is an example of a poem that does two things at once: it gives the sun and moon imaginary human qualities; and it contains information and facts about the sun and moon. Read the poem aloud line-by-line, and ask the children to try and identify the facts. Highlight or chart all the facts and information they can learn from this poem. Then encourage children to write their own nonfiction poems about things in the world about which they're experts.

Thursday: Poet's Talk

Poet Bobbi Katz tells us that she often needs to

"do some research . . . some of my poems are based on history or science.
I always try my very best to get the facts straight."

Let me read Bobbi Katz's poem "Sun and Moon: A Poem for Two Voices" to you again. Let's listen for the ideas in her poem that are based on science and "getting her facts straight."

Friday: Craft Talk

◎ The poet uses **two voices** to help us contrast the two perspectives. This is a relatively simple structure that many young writers will use with great success.

◎ The poet also uses **line breaks** and **white space** to make a visual distinction between the two voices. This helps us distinguish between the two and helps us read their voices differently.

◎ The poet uses **personification** to write what the sun and the moon might say to each other if they could. Personification means putting on the "mask" of something or someone else and speaking in that voice—it usually refers to situations where things that aren't human are given human traits. A poem written in that voice is called a **persona poem**. Children will enjoy trying this out and writing from the perspectives of objects in their everyday lives or in the world in general.

Singing Down the Sun

Starlings gather in the trees
    three by two by one.
Wheedling, tweedling, shreedling,
    singing down the sun.
Each evening it's the same old game.
    They think it's lots of fun.
Bristling, whistling, shristling
    till the day is done,
    thinking they have won,
      singing down the sun.

– By Marilyn Singer

Singing Down the Sun
Marilyn Singer

Monday: Introduce the Poem (big book page 32)

The Heart of the Poem

*The way words sound can be a really important part of a poem—like in "Singing Down the Sun,"
by Marilyn Singer. The poet notices how birds called starlings gather in trees each day at sunset,
making a big racket! The poet imagines that the birds think their singing causes the sun to set. Listen
to how the poet uses sound words to describe the birds' song.*

Conversations About the Poem

*Let's list the sound words that Marilyn Singer used to describe the starlings' song at sunset. Some of
the words might even be made up—that's another exciting thing that poets get to do sometimes!*

Tuesday: Ways to Climb Inside the Poem

Illustrating

Ask children to close their eyes as they listen to the poem again and try to make the
mind-pictures from the words in the poem. What mind-pictures do they see? Have
a conversation about the materials that would help them best record these mind-
pictures. Gather the materials and ask children to draw the mind-pictures they saw
to post around the poem for the week. Materials might include an assortment of
papers, watercolor paints, tissue paper, pastels, chalk, and crayons.

Choral Reading

Read the poem aloud once to model the pace and cadence. Then invite the entire
class to read along with you for one reading. Next try to create the effect of a lower-
ing sun. Divide the class into four groups and give this a try:

Poem	Readers
Starlings gather in the trees three by two by one.	Groups 1, 2, 3, 4
Wheedling, tweedling, shreedling, singing down the sun.	Groups 1, 2, 3, 4
Each evening it's the same old game. They think it's lots of fun.	Groups 1, 2, 3, 4
Bristling,	Group 1
whistling,	Group 2
shristling	Group 3
till the day is done,	Group 4
thinking they have won,	Groups 1, 2, 3, 4 [lower the volume on each
singing down the sun.	line to whisper the last line]

Wednesday: Ways to Climb Inside the Poem

Interactive Writing

Sound can be a very important part of a poem. Write your own sound poem together about the sounds you hear while sitting together in your very own classroom. Ask your students to sit silently with their eyes closed for a minute or two, just listening. Remind them how full of sounds the world is, and that part of a poet's job is to pay attention to every little detail, including the sounds. When your moments of silent listening end, simply list the noises your students heard. Encourage them to use descriptive sound words as Marilyn Singer did in her poem. You may even invite them to make up their own sound words.

Thursday: Poet's Talk

Marilyn Singer says,

> "A good poem . . . uses words wonderfully, and it uses them to capture specific moments in a fresh way, a way that makes the reader exclaim with delight, 'Yes, that's it! That's right!'"

Let me read you her poem "Singing Down the Sun" once again, and let's listen for those ways that Marilyn Singer "uses words wonderfully."

Friday: Craft Talk

- The poet uses **sound words** to describe the birdsong heard at the end of the day. Poets often use all of their senses to describe an experience. Practicing using each of the senses will be fun for young poets and will help them add a variety of details to their poems.

- The poet also uses **made-up words** to describe exactly what the birds sound like. This can be a fun, playful activity for young poets who love wordplay.

Hey, Crow!

Your cackle cuts the air,
a black laugh
meant to scare me,
but I won't be bullied
by your feathered cape,
flapping in that
twisted tree.
Think I believe
your sorcery?

Halloween is gone,
you fraud
hiding with
that cape and cough—
go and take your
costume off!

— By Deborah Chandra

Hey, Crow!
Deborah Chandra

Monday: Introduce the Poem (big book page 33)

The Heart of the Poem

Sometimes we talk to our pets or other animals as if they were people. We say things to them as if they understand what we are saying. The speaker in the poem is talking to the crow instead of about it. The speaker also imagines that the crow is dressed up and pretending to be scary even though Halloween is gone! Close your eyes as I read, and see what mind-pictures you make from the words in the poem.

Conversations About the Poem

What did you see in your mind? Turn and share your mind-pictures with the person next to you. Were your mind-pictures like the ideas in the poem? How were they different?

Tuesday: Ways to Climb Inside the Poem

Shared Reading

Read the poem to your class once or twice to set the tone, pace, and intensity. Let your voice show the playful, teasing feeling between the poet and the crow. Then read the poem together in unison.

Choral Reading

Read the poem and ask children to think of and make sound effects that match the words. For example:

Poem	Sound
Your cackle cuts the air, a black laugh . . .	cackling
by your feathered cape, flapping . . .	flapping sounds
hiding with that cape and cough . . .	flapping and cackling

Wednesday: Ways to Climb Inside the Poem

Interactive Writing

Choose an animal to write to in the same way that the poet writes to a crow. You may choose to write about a pigeon or squirrel or some other animal that children might be able to see together from the window of your classroom, to help make the poem feel more immediate. What do you say to this animal? If you want to expand on this idea, you might add another stanza in which the animal chooses to speak back to you!

Thursday: Poet's Talk

Deborah Chandra, the poet of "Hey, Crow!" is a second-grade teacher. She says,

"Often [students] bring objects to school for sharing. One day P.J. brings a fuzzy sycamore leaf, another day Bryan brings his lost tooth . . . Ireyna, her pet tarantula. All these objects the children have 'looked upon' and now hold up at sharing as if they held a touch of majesty . . . What seems like a familiar fact takes on a magical freshness. Bryan holds his lost tooth above his head as if it glowed like a rising moon."

I'm thinking of Deborah Chandra's poem "Hey, Crow!" and how an ordinary crow takes on a "magical freshness" in her poem. If we look at her poem again, where in the poem does she bring the magical freshness to describe the ordinary crow?

Friday: Craft Talk

- ◎ The poet speaks directly to the crow in this poem. When poets address a poem to an object or person, it's called an **apostrophe poem**.

- ◎ The poet uses **metaphor** (or comparison) to describe the crow's wings—they are not just wings, they are a "feathered cape."

- ◎ The poet creates strong **images**, as when she describes the way the crow's caw "cuts the air."

Hidden Treasure

At night the city shows its treasures,
flashing diamond necklaces,
glittering rubies
     and
green emeralds
that days disguise
as bridges and traffic lights.

     – By Bobbi Katz

Hidden Treasure
Bobbi Katz

Monday: Introduce the Poem (big book page 34)

The Heart of the Poem

Poets often paint pictures in the minds of readers by comparing one thing to another thing. As I read this poem, you will hear the poet describing beautiful jewels—think hard about what the poet might really be talking about.

Conversations About the Poem

Turn and tell the person next to you what you think Bobbi Katz was really writing about when she described the "treasures" the city displays at night.

Sometimes comparing one thing to something that is similar in some way can help us see the world in a way we've never thought of before. Now close your eyes and imagine your own city or town at night. How might you describe the lights of your city by comparing them to something that is similar in some way? Let's list some ideas together.

Tuesday: Ways to Climb Inside the Poem

Illustrating

Have children begin with black paper and white crayons to create the outline of the cityscape. Provide sequins, glitter, and bits of cellophane or tissue paper to create the city's "jewels" at night. If this feels too labor-intensive, simply using oil pastels on black construction paper can also create the effect of the city at night. Read the poem aloud as the artists are working. Hang a copy of the poem next to the children's art.

Wednesday: Ways to Climb Inside the Poem

Interactive Writing

Write "At night . . ." on a sheet of chart paper, and ask children to close their eyes and get their own mind-pictures of what they see outside at night. Have them share with one another first, and then share in the larger group. Write down what they say to create a class poem about night.

Thursday: Poet's Talk

Bobbi Katz says,

> "Ideas are everywhere, if we only let ourselves slow down enough to observe the world around us and within us."

I can imagine that Bobbi Katz slowed down enough to look at the night sky in New York City, where she lives, and then found "hidden treasure" where most people would just see city lights. Let's read her poem again, and think about what the poet is observing. Which ideas come from the world around her? Which ideas come from the "world within"?

Friday: Craft Talk

- The poet uses strong **images** to help us visualize the city at night. Words like "flashing diamond necklace" and "glittering rubies" and "green emeralds" help us to see the color and think about the lights as the "jewels" of the city.

- The poet uses **metaphor** (or comparison) to describe the lights of her city at night; instead of just writing about the lights, she compares them to sparkling jewels.

- The poet also uses the **line breaks** and **white space** to set off each image as a phrase unto itself. That helps us think of each image one at a time and causes us to read each line as a distinct phrase.

- The **title** of the poem, "Hidden Treasure," is not just a label but extends the poem's meaning.

Night Story

When the blue page of day
Is turned to night,
An alphabet of stars
Is printed, small and bright,
On dark and ancient-storied skies—

We read the universe
With wondering eyes.

– By Beverly McLoughland

Night Story
Beverly McLoughland

Monday: Introduce the Poem (big book page 35)

The Heart of the Poem
We have all been outside as the day slowly turns to night. We have seen the stars begin to shine. In this poem, the poet reminds us of that time of day and describes the sky and stars in some unexpected ways.

Conversations About the Poem
How did the poet describe the sky and the stars in this poem? Talk with your neighbor about why a poet would choose to title this poem "Night Story," and why the poet would say we can "read the universe." Are the universe and the stars like a story? What is the story of the universe and the stars? Let's share some of those ideas.

Tuesday: Ways to Climb Inside the Poem

Choral Reading
Read the poem aloud to set a pace. Note that the poem is one sentence broken into phrase units with line breaks and white space. Remember to pause slightly on the end of each line. Ask everyone to join in on the final line.

Illustrating
This poem uses such vivid mind-pictures, or images, that it's easy to picture. As you read the poem aloud, ask children to close their eyes and try to see the images of the poem. Ask them to draw the images they saw in their minds, and then have them explain their drawings when the class is finished.

Wednesday: Ways to Climb Inside the Poem

Interactive Writing
Some of the most powerful poems can also be some of the shortest. The poet uses very few words to explore some very big ideas in the poem "Night Story," and metaphor helps expand the ideas of the poem. Help your children practice the art of

metaphor-making by collaborating on their own poem about the night sky. Brainstorm a short list of things they might see in the night sky (moon, stars, sky, clouds, glowing streetlight, and so on). Then have your students come up with comparisons for each of these things. You may give them some prompts—for example, "What do the stars remind you of?" You may choose to use the list of night-sky objects the children have generated by writing them out as sentence-starters on your chart paper:

Night is . . .

The stars are . . .

The moon is . . .

Use as many different comparison ideas as your children come up with to fill in the blanks; there's no need to limit each element of the night to one comparison.

Thursday: Poet's Talk

Beverly McLougland writes that for her,

"Many [poems] come from my sense of wonder and curiosity about animals and the natural world. The two poems in this book began that way. . . . 'Night Story' came about from looking up at the stars and wondering about them."

Can't you just feel Beverly McLoughland's sense of wonder at the night sky in her poem, "Night Story"? Where do you sense her wonder in the poem?

Friday: Craft Talk

- ◉ The poet uses **metaphor**, comparing the sky to a page ("blue page of day") and the stars to letters in the alphabet ("An alphabet of stars") to help the reader imagine the sky as a book that can be read.
- ◉ The poet uses the first-person **point of view**, "we," to create a personal and inclusive tone.
- ◉ The poet uses a **stanza break** to let the reader pause before the last two ending lines.

Poets

Poet Profiles: Getting to Know the Featured Poets

Alice Schertle has said, "A cherished poem is a gift that we may carry with us all our lives." Now think of how that cherished gift may be even more treasured when we feel that we know the creator of the gift—the poet. The following section includes profiles of the poets featured in the *Climb Inside a Poem* big book. These profiles will help you and your students make connections to the poems and expand your thinking about being a poet. Each profile includes:

◎ **Biographical information** that you may want to share with your students, especially if they are interested in a particular poet. Decide which information will be most relevant to your students, and share it with them. The poet's web address, when available, is included.

◎ **Tips for young writers** from the poet. Here, the poet has shared his or her thoughts about a variety of topics: finding ideas for writing, finding the best place to work, making time for writing, choosing the right tools for writing, and so on. Often, we have provided a discussion question or writing suggestion that follows up on the poet's words.

◎ **A list of each poet's work**, including the poems contributed to *Climb Inside a Poem* and other published work that is particularly appropriate for young children.

As you climb inside the poems and delve into the work of writing poetry with your students, we invite you to make the experience even more personal by helping your young poets see the many things they have in common with these great poets. Prior to introducing a poem by a particular poet, you might show children the photo of the poet, share a few tidbits from the biography, and read a few of the Poet-to-Poet notes. This introduction will help children make a more personal connection to the poet and to the poem. After children are familiar with the poem, you could revisit the profile to help them get a deeper sense of how the poet works or what he or she likes to write about.

Additionally, as you prepare to carry out a reading or writing minilesson from the *Reading and Writing Poetry Across the Year* guidebook, you might want to read any of the profiles that will provide support to your minilesson. Many minilessons include quotes from these poets and Book Links to works they have published.

Joseph Bruchac

"Read poems . . . Then start writing down your own words. Keep doing it. Keep doing it. Keep doing it."

Getting to Know Joseph Bruchac

Joseph Bruchac lives in Greenfield Center, New York, in the same house where he was raised by his grandparents. His grandmother kept their house full of books and always encouraged him to read poetry. As a result, he was writing poems for his teachers by the time he was in second grade. Joseph Bruchac's writing often reflects and celebrates his Abenaki Indian ancestry.

Joseph Bruchac married his wife Carol in 1964, and they went to live in Ghana, West Africa, for three years as volunteers. Mr. Bruchac taught English there. When they returned to the United States, they founded an award-winning poetry magazine, *The Greenfield Review*, which they published for 18 years. Joseph Bruchac's poems have appeared in more than 500 magazine and anthologies. He is the author of over 30 books of his own poetry and editor of more than a dozen books of poetry by other writers. Mr. Bruchac has been a professional writer and storyteller since 1981. He has given storytelling performances across the United States and Europe and also taught writing workshops in many schools.

To find out more about Joseph Bruchac, visit www.josephbruchac.com.

Poet to Poet: Tips for Young Writers

Finding Ideas for Writing

Joseph Bruchac says,

"The ideas for my poems almost always begin with a phrase, a few words that come into my head. Of course, those words are usually in response to something I have dreamed or experienced or seen. For example, I look outside and see a male cardinal perched on the side window of my car, trying to fight his own reflection in the mirror. Then these words come to mind:

The cardinal has a quarrel with himself

(I write them down and then just keep writing, seeing where the image and the words take me.)

> he taps and taps against the mirror
> trying to drive away the other,
> an ugly and determined bird
> that meets his attack, blow for blow.
>
> You see he doesn't know
> what you and I must also learn—
> Your worst enemy is your ego.
> (And there it is—a new poem.)
> What inspires me to write a poem? It is this business of living, life itself."

Wow, we just heard Joseph Bruchac write a poem. I wonder if we could do that. Perhaps we should give that a try. What's an image we can start with? What words come to mind? Let's see if our words can become a poem, too.

Finding the Best Place to Work

When Joseph Bruchac was asked where he likes to write, he said,

> "Much of my writing takes place in my study—a small room I have set aside in our cabin—where I am away from the phone . . . What makes a place suitable for me for writing is that it is somewhere where I will not be disturbed."

It sounds as if Joseph Bruchac is like some of us when he writes. He wants to be away from distractions. He likes for it to be quiet, and he doesn't want to be interrupted. Does that sound like you?

Advice for Young Poets

What does Joseph Bruchac suggest for someone who wants to get better at writing? He says,

> "Read poems by great writers—from the past and the present."

Several of our poet friends have suggested that reading a lot of poems will help make you a better writer. That is one reason we read poetry every day. It helps to strengthen our "writing muscles."

Poems in *Climb Inside a Poem*

"The Cedar Tree"

Read More by Joseph Bruchac

Thirteen Moons on Turtle's Back
   Putnam Juvenile reprint edition, 1997
The Earth Under Sky Bear's Feet
   Philomel, 1995
Many Nations: An Alphabet of Native America
   Scholastic, 2004
Between Earth and Sky: Legends of Native American Sacred Places
   Voyager Books reprint edition, 1999
Seasons of the Circle: A Native American Year
   Troll Communications, 2002

Deborah Chandra

"Sometimes kids talk poetry to each other without knowing it."

Getting to Know Deborah Chandra

Deborah Chandra was born and brought up in a small town in California. Her home was near the San Gabriel Mountains, and she spent a lot of time exploring the trails and canyons.

When she grew up, Deborah Chandra became a teacher and studied poetry with a famous poet named Myra Cohn Livingstone. Ms. Chandra says, "We all need someone—older and wiser—to pat us on the back and tell us we're not crazy after all. Myra was that someone for me."

Deborah Chandra has won several honors and awards for her poetry.

Poet to Poet: Tips for Young Writers

Finding Ideas for Writing

Deborah Chandra says that her second-grade students bring objects for sharing—a fuzzy sycamore leaf, a lost tooth, even a pet tarantula. Her students are like you; they notice the beauty and wonder in all the amazing things in the world, big and small. The children help her remember to look at the marvelous and miraculous in the things of this world. That is what we should do; we should notice the amazing things in the world around us and think of the poetry we could write from that.

Advice for Young Poets

If you want to see your writing get better and better, here's what Deborah Chandra suggests:

"Get acquainted with lots of words; they are your tools. Have fun with their sounds—turn them round on your tongue, feel them bump and hiss and slip, and notice how different speech sounds make you feel . . . The thoughts and feelings inside us rely on the right words in order to show themselves through poetry."

Finding Time for Writing

Some writers work on their writing every day. But some writers, like Deborah Chandra, have other jobs as well. Ms. Chandra also teaches second grade, so she spends every day at school, just like we do. How does she find time for writing? She says,

> "I don't have a strict routine. How I wish I did! Teaching full-time is a big job and writing poems often has to be put aside. Yet poetry is found in students' textbooks, library books, I fill the classroom with it, and through my days I hear the words of the wonderful poets who have entered my life—some have come centuries after they lived. Their works have a way of talking to me, laughing, chattering, whispering, howling, gossiping. I have collected them, and they are constantly with me."

Poems in *Climb Inside a Poem*

"Hey, Crow!"

Read More by Deborah Chandra

Balloons: And Other Poems
Farrar, Straus and Giroux reprint edition, 2006
Rich Lizard: And Other Poems
Sunburst, 1996
Miss Mabel's Table
Harcourt, 1994
Who Comes?
Sierra Club Books for Children, 1995
A Is for Amos
Farrar, Straus and Giroux, 1999
George Washington's Teeth
Farrar, Straus and Giroux, 2003

Rebecca Kai Dotlich

"I love finding the right words. The stupendous, the magnificent, and the ordinary words. I collect them."

"Poetry matters because it holds the key. The key to our heart, to our inner voice, to our soul."

Getting to Know Rebecca Kai Dotlich

Rebecca Kai Dotlich has two grown children, one grandchild, and another grandchild soon to be born. She lives with her husband in Indiana. She *doesn't* live in a rambling old farmhouse or in a cottage by the sea. She *is* able to see, from her writing room window, a stream that meanders past her backyard.

Rebecca Kai Dotlich is a poet and picture book author. Her work has been featured on *Reading Rainbow*, published in magazines such as *Ladybug* and *Highlights for Children*, and included in several books and collections. Her work has won several awards, and she speaks at conferences, retreats, libraries, and schools across the country. Ms. Dotlich has also been a poetry advisor and columnist for two magazines for teachers, *Creative Classroom* and *Teaching Pre K–8*.

To find out more about Rebecca Kai Dotlich, visit www.rebeccakaidotlich.com.

Poet to Poet: Tips for Young Writers

Finding Ideas for Writing

Rebecca Kai Dotlich says that the inspiration for a poem can happen in a million ways. Sometimes it comes in something she hears being said. It might be funny or serious, and it doesn't matter if it catches her as a rhythmic or snappy or even enchanting line. When it happens, she scribbles out that one line and works with it. Sometimes an image sparks an idea. That image might be the old, twisted part of a tree where the wood is gnarled; or the way a baseball sails in the sky; or the way a ladybug tenderly makes her way from leaf to limb. Sometimes she gets an idea from looking at the illustrations in books of poetry or from a memory sparked by a smell or sound. Rebecca Kai Dotlich says that ideas for poetry are everywhere. Ideas are everywhere. So let's be on the lookout for them today and every day. When you notice something that sparks an idea for a poem or some other writing, you can let us know, and we will write it on our class chart of great ideas for writing.

Finding the Best Place to Work

Does Rebecca Kai Dotlich have a favorite place to write? She says,

"I absolutely have a favorite place to write—in my writing room, which used to be an extra bedroom of the house. It has a wall of bookshelves, a light green and pink couch, a rolltop desk, filing drawers, a fax, a copier, and a long wall of corkboard to pin up favorite photographs, cards, postcards, comic strips, quotations, and letters from children. There is a window that overlooks the backyard with pear trees and a small stream. In this room are many of my favorite things (besides all of my poetry, biographies, and picture books). There are books that my brother and I had when we were young, clay sculptures my children made in grade school, small toys and comic books, lots of framed pictures, paperweights, etc. Of course I write in other places; my back porch, an airplane, a hotel room, a coffee shop . . . but only in snatches. I'll make notes and brainstorm and cobble together a first draft, but no other place feels as right to get a poem or any piece of writing to the finished stage."

Whoa, poets, did you notice all the details Ms. Dotlich gave us when she described her special writing room? She helped us see her writing room with the words she chose. That must be a special place to her. Her special writing room gives me an idea. Maybe we can make some special places in our room for writers to go when they have a few free moments to work on a poem. What would we need to put in that special writing space? What do writers need to have near them when they are getting down to the work of writing? Let's think about that for a moment.

Advice for Young Poets

When Rebecca Kai Dotlich was asked for her advice to young poets, she said,

"Always, find wonder in your world. Look—really look at that frog near the pond, that bus rumbling down the road, that sunflower towering over the fence, that puddle shimmering in the field, that tiny paper clip on the desk. Open your eyes and your heart to all the senses, all the imaginings, all the words and images in the world."

Ms. Dotlich is reminding us once again to pay attention to the details in the world around us, to notice the little things that most people just walk right by. That's good advice.

Poems in *Climb Inside a Poem*

"Sky Wish"
"Birthday Candles"

Read More by Rebecca Kai Dotlich

"Paper Clips"
> (in the *Reading and Writing Poetry Across the Year* guidebook)

Sweet Dreams of the Wild: Poems for Bedtime
> Boyds Mills Press, 2000

Lemonade Sun: And Other Summer Poems
> Boyds Mills Press, 1998

When Riddles Come Rumbling: Poems to Ponder
> Boyds Mills Press, 2001

In the Spin of Things: Poetry of Motion
> Boyds Mills Press, 2003

Over in the Pink House: New Jump-Rope Rhymes
> Boyds Mills Press, 2004

What Is Science?
> Henry Holt, 2006

Kristine O'Connell George

"Many of my poems are about things I love so much that I feel I have to write about them."

"There's a certain private joy in finding an image or a handful of words that perfectly captures what I want to say."

Getting to Know Kristine O'Connell George

Kristine O'Connell George was born in Denver, Colorado, and her family moved often when she was growing up. She says that memories of her homes in Colorado, Idaho, Ohio, Oregon, Texas, and California are sources of inspiration for her poetry.

Now Kristine O'Connell George lives with her family in the Santa Monica Mountains of southern California. She says that she often finds poetry in her own backyard. "The owl roosting in our 300-year-old native oak, the packs of coyotes howling at night, the neighborhood peacocks, and the frog who lives on our front porch all seem to find their way into my work. Someday, I think I'll write about the raccoon who played with the dog's toys in the yard at 2 A.M. Or the skunk family . . ."

Kristine O'Connell George says she fell in love with poetry in 1989, when she was taking a children's poetry writing class taught by a famous poet named Myra Cohn Livingston. Ms. George and her poetry have won many awards and honors. She is a frequent speaker at conferences. She also enjoys visiting schools, conducting poetry workshops, and sharing her enthusiasm for poetry with students of all ages.

To find out more about Kristine O'Connell George, visit www.kristinegeorge.com.

Poet to Poet: Tips for Young Writers

Finding Ideas for Writing

Kristine O'Connell George says,

> "Ideas for my poems arrive in surprising and almost always unexpected ways. I might overhear (or mishear) something which sends my mind wandering. Or, I might look at something ordinary and see it in a new way: a monkey wrench looks as if it has a face. Ideas for poems arrive when my heart is touched deeply in some way. Many of my poems are about things I love so much that I feel I have to write about them."

Finding the Best Place to Work

Many of us have one or two favorite spots where we like to write. Well, so does Kristine O'Connell George. Her favorite place is sitting in a big chair on her back patio with her feet up. She says,

"I'm trying to learn to write in different places . . . If I'm traveling, I like to find a park bench or somewhere outside to write."

You might have a favorite place in our room where you like to work on your writing, but maybe we should try her suggestion and write outside one day. We could sit on the playground, on a bench, or on the sidewalk. I wonder if we would write differently outside. Let's try that one day. Oh, and there's one more thing Kristine O'Connell George says about where she writes:

"I also do a lot of writing 'in my head' as I go about my day."

Have you ever thought about that? Writing in your head—isn't that an interesting idea? We do that, too, don't we? We get an idea and just say a poem. Remember the minilesson we had on "noticing poetry in what we say"? Well, that is like writing in your head. You have to think it and then say it, and then we write it. So we are like Kristine O'Connell George; we do write in our heads sometimes.

Choosing the Right Tools for Writing

We love our special paper and our favorite pens, pencils, and markers. We love our notebooks and sticky notes. It seems that many writers are like us. Kristine O'Connell George says that she loves to go in office supply stores because she likes all the different kinds of paper and pens and pencils. She says,

"I'm constantly experimenting with new ways to write: poem snippets on index cards or Post-It notes. Different types of notebooks. A variety of pens and pencils . . . Right now, I'm writing in large artist tablets and enjoy using the expanse of space to scribble, sketch, and toss words all over a large sheet of paper. I rarely start a poem on a computer; even if I eventually do type the poem, I print it out and wander off somewhere to read and think about it and edit."

Poems in *Climb Inside a Poem*

"Dear Friend in the Desert"
"How I Hopscotch"

Read More by Kristine O'Connell George

Fold Me a Poem
    Harcourt, 2005
Up!
    Clarion Books, 2005
Hummingbird Nest: A Journal of Poems
    Harcourt, 2004
Little Dog and Duncan
    Clarion Books, 2002
Little Dog Poems
    Clarion Books, 1999
Toasting Marshmallows: Camping Poems
    Clarion Books, 2001
Old Elm Speaks: Tree Poems
    Clarion Books reprint edition, 2007
The Great Frog Race: And Other Poems
    Clarion Books reprint edition, 2005

Georgia Heard

"Poetry is really everywhere—especially surprising places—where most people wouldn't think of looking."

Getting to Know Georgia Heard

Georgia Heard went to college at Columbia University in New York City, where she also taught poetry to children in the New York City schools. She was so inspired by the poems that the children wrote, she wrote a book about what she learned. She titled it *For the Good of the Earth and Sun*—and dedicated it: *for the kids of the New York City schools*. Since then she's traveled all over the United States, Canada, the Middle East, Southeast Asia, and Europe teaching poetry.

When she's not writing and teaching, Georgia Heard loves taking long walks with her son and husband. She and her family like to travel and meet different people from around the world.

Poet to Poet: Tips for Young Writers

Advice for Young Poets

Here is Georgia Heard's advice to young poets:

- ◎ Speak in your natural voice, as if you were talking to your best friend.
- ◎ Write down your observations.
- ◎ Be a word collector—collect words you love in a notebook.
- ◎ Don't be afraid to write down what you really think and feel—there are people who feel the same way as you do.

Finding Ideas for Writing

Georgia Heard says that her poems often start with

"observations that make my heart open and help me see the world, and my life, in a new way."

Finding the Best Place to Work
Georgia Heard says,

> "A poem can begin anywhere—on a plane, in the airport, in a car, waiting in line
> at the grocery store, at school, or at home. That's why keeping a notebook with
> me at all times is important so I don't miss a poem that might want to be written
> at that very moment."

Poems in *Climb Inside a Poem*

"Where Do I Find Poetry?"

Read More by Georgia Heard

Creatures of Earth, Sea, and Sky
   Boyds Mills Press, 1997
Songs of Myself: An Anthology of Poems and Art
   Mondo, 2001
This Place I Know: Poems of Comfort
   Candlewick, 2002, reissued 2006
Falling Down the Page: List Poems
   Roaring Brook Press, 2008

Lee Bennett Hopkins

"The best part of writing poetry is . . . trying to pare down thoughts in a few—but wonderfully, magically, chosen words."

Getting to Know Lee Bennett Hopkins

Lee Bennett Hopkins has written many poems and books for children and adults. His poetry autobiography, *Been to Yesterdays*, won a Christopher Award and a Golden Kite Honor. To encourage other poets, he created the Lee Bennett Hopkins Award for Children's Poetry and the Lee Bennett Hopkins Promising Poet Award.

Mr. Hopkins has written and collected poems about many topics. His poetry books include *Marvelous Math*, *Spectacular Science,* and *Lives: Poems About Famous Americans*. His book for teachers, *Pass the Poetry, Please!,* has been in print for over 25 years.

Lee Bennett Hopkins has received the University of Southern Mississippi's Medallion for "lasting contributions to children's literature." Mr. Hopkins lives in Westchester County, New York, and Cape Coral, Florida.

Poet to Poet: Tips for Young Writers

Finding Ideas for Writing

We have talked a lot about where we get ideas for our writing. Lee Bennett Hopkins says,

"Ideas seem to just come—at the most unexpected times. Something inside my head seems to say: 'Write a poem about me! I need attention!' So I try to do the subject justice—be it a watering can or a sparrow."

Isn't that interesting, an idea seems to ask him to write about it. Mmm, I wonder if you've ever felt that an idea was just tugging at you, wanting you to write about it. Let's think about that this week. Let's pay attention to the ideas that come to us and see if any of them seem to be asking us to write.

Advice for Young Poets

Lots of poets have given us advice about becoming a better writer. Several of them said we needed to read lots of poems if we want to write poems. Lee Bennett Hopkins says that and more.

"If you want to write poetry, READ poetry. And practice, practice, practice. Do not accept first, third, or even fifth drafts. Writing is REWRITING. Learn your craft as you would if you wanted to be a baseball player or a rap singer."

So, we need to read lots of poems and notice what the poets are doing. We do that each week, don't we? That means we are growing as poets every week, as we read more poems and study how the poet did his or her work. And did you hear Mr. Hopkins's other suggestion—we need to write a lot? "Practice, practice, practice," he said. Did you notice what he said about baseball players or rap singers? They don't get to be really good unless they practice. Well, that is why we write so many poems ourselves. We are growing as poets each week.

Poems in *Climb Inside a Poem*

"Tooth Truth"
"Why? Why? Why?"

Read More by Lee Bennett Hopkins

Days to Celebrate: A Full Year of Poetry, People, Holidays, History, Fascinating Facts, and More
    Greenwillow, 2004
Wonderful Words: Poems About Reading, Writing, Speaking, and Listening
    Simon and Schuster, 2004
Sports! Sports! Sports! A Poetry Collection
    HarperCollins, 1999
Alphathoughts: Alphabet Poems
    Boyds Mills Press, 2003
Questions: Poems (I Can Read)
    HarperTrophy, 1994
Best Friends
    HarperCollins, 1986
Side by Side: Poems to Read Together
    Simon and Schuster, 1988
Spectacular Science: A Book of Poems
    Aladdin, reprint edition, 2002
Behind the Museum Door: Poems to Celebrate the Wonders of Museums
    Abrams Books, 2007
Lives: Poems About Famous Americans
    HarperCollins, 1999

Patricia Hubbell

"Poetry writing helps you to share your feelings and to make yourself known in a new way."

Getting to Know Patricia Hubbell

Patricia Hubbell grew up in the little town of Easton, Connecticut—and now, almost eighty years later, she still lives there. She started writing poems in the third grade. She wrote them on pieces of cardboard that came from the laundry in her father's freshly ironed shirts. Sometimes, she took one of her poems to school, and the teacher read it to the class. Ms. Hubbell says she thinks she started writing poems because her mother and grandmother read poetry to her from the time she was very small. She thinks those word pictures and rhythms got down inside her somehow and made her able to write her own poems.

Pat Hubbell has two grown children named Deborah and Jeff, one granddaughter named Megan, and two step-granddaughters named Shoshana and Shira. She says, "Today, my husband and I live in a modern house with lots of glass, which looks out at woods, a pond, and our barn. There are no horses in the barn anymore, and I have turned the paddock into a garden. It is still nice, but in a different way. I do art work and crafts, work in my garden, go to restaurants and take day-trips with my husband. We read a lot, visit our children and grandchildren, and I often talk to groups of schoolchildren. Of course, I still like to write poetry!"

To find out more about Patricia Hubbell, you can visit her website at www.kidspoet.com

Poet to Poet: Tips for Young Writers

Finding Ideas for Writing

Pat Hubbell says that many things get her started writing poems. It might be a sound, a rhythm, a word, or something she has seen or experienced. But something needs to capture her attention. Then she feels a little "tug" in her mind and she knows a poem is about to begin. She says,

> "Looking for poem subjects is a bit like going fishing—you wait for the tug on the line and then you reel in your catch—not a fish, but a poem!"

Wow, fishing for poems. That's an interesting idea. Can you think of ways we might go fishing for poems? If we read several poems, will that help us "catch" an idea? If we take a walk outside, will that help us "catch" a poem? Let's think about that for a minute.

Advice for Young Poets

Patricia Hubbell gives this advice to young poets:

> "Pay attention to everything. Ask questions, study, look closely, examine. Notice details—is the bird a robin or a thrush? Is the stone quartz or granite? Details make the poem strong."

We know that details make strong poems, don't we? Let's take a look at some of our favorite poems and see how the details make the poems strong. Do the details help us know exactly what the poet is writing about? Do they help us hear sounds and notice movements?

Finding Time for Writing

Pat Hubbell says,

> "My writing routine is apt to change according to what I have to do during the day. But in general, I get up a little before six, have breakfast, and sit down to work. Sometimes that means writing new things, sometimes revising. Sometimes it's thinking, or researching, or just making word lists. Sometimes, if I want to write a poem but haven't felt the 'tug,' I'll read poetry for an hour or so. That really gets me in the mood to write! The poems' words, images, sounds, help me to fill my mind with my own images, sounds, and rhythms, and all at once I'm in a poetry-writing mood. If I have a relatively free day ahead, I may stay at my desk for three or four hours or more. If I have a busy day ahead, I may only fit in an hour or so."

Wow, did you know that writers did so much work? Writing new things, revising, thinking, researching, and reading—all of those things are part of a writer's work. Do we do all that work when we are writing? Let's think about that. We write new things, right? And we revise a lot, don't we? We certainly do a lot of thinking and reading, and we do research new ideas all through the day. So, what do you think? Do we write like Patricia Hubbell?

Poems in *Climb Inside a Poem*

"When I Ride My Bike"
"Poem for My Friend"
"Song for My Swing"

Read More by Patricia Hubbell

Rabbit Moon: A Book of Holidays and Celebrations
    Marshall Cavendish, 2002

Black Earth, Gold Sun
    Marshall Cavendish, 2001

Earthmates: Poems
    Marshall Cavendish, 2000

Hurray For Spring!
    NorthWord, 2005

Trains: Steaming! Pulling! Huffing!
    Marshall Cavendish, 2005

Black All Around!
    Lee & Low Books, 2003

Bobbi Katz

"Ideas are everywhere, if we only let ourselves slow down enough to observe the world around us and within us."

Getting to Know Bobbi Katz

Bobbi Katz says that her love affair with rhyme and rhythm began when she realized that letters on her alphabet blocks could be grouped together to *mean* something. Her parents both worked six long days every week, but the family had a live-in house-keeper, Emmy, whom Bobbi pestered to "read" to her. She wasn't asking for stories— she just wanted to see and hear the labels on the items in the pantry: PEACHES, TUNA FISH, BAKING SODA, AMMONIA. These words became her playmates! She remembers clapping and dancing around with them, making up rhymes:

> *Ammonia begonia, who's gonna phone 'ya?*
> *Ammonia begonia, who will it be?*
> *Peaches can't do it 'cause they're stuck in a can.*
> *Who's gonna phone 'ya?*
> *The Tuna Fish man!*
> *The T-U-N-A Tuna Fish man. . . .*

Bobbi Katz says she never lost her delight in language. Words are still her playmates.

Bobbi Katz even remembers the very first time that "write a poem" was a school assignment. That was in sixth grade, and the subject was the discovery of bronze. Bobbi Katz says that teacher gave her "permission" to write poetry.

Now Ms. Katz divides her time between New York City and a small apartment in upstate New York, right on the Hudson River. She loves music, dancing the salsa, and walking along the river, in the woods, or on the city streets. She studies astronomy, which makes our planet, Earth, seem all the more precious.

To find out more about Bobbi Katz, visit www.bobbikatz.com.

Poet to Poet: Tips for Young Writers

Finding Ideas for Writing
If you have ever wondered where to get ideas for your poems, you might listen to what Bobbi Katz says:

"Ideas are everywhere, if we only let ourselves slow down enough to observe the world around us and within us."

She says that her poems come from all over the place:

"Sights, sounds, memories, tastes, touch, and even National Public Radio!"

So the next time you are wondering what to write about, maybe you should take a few minutes to get really quiet and listen and get really still and look around you. There may be a great idea right there with you.

Finding Time for Writing

Writers do a lot of work that readers never see. Just listen to how Bobbi Katz spends her day:

"Usually I start the day about 8:00 A.M. with yoga or a walk; then I drink a cup of tea with lots of skim milk and start to write. I take a break in a few hours for a big breakfast: usually a gigantic salad with foods of many different colors. Then I might return to writing or do some research. Even though I love to write funny poems and poems about what I experience, some of my poems are based on history or science. I always try my very best to get the facts straight. That means trying to find copies of original letters or documents, not what someone said that someone said that someone said."

Did you know that some of the work of a writer is to read and do research to find documents and resources? Writers can be very busy people.

Choosing the Right Tools for Writing

Most of the time in school we write in our notebooks or on paper. Bobbi Katz says,

"I write directly on my computer. And rewrite. And rewrite."

Did you hear that part about rewriting? That is an important part of making your writing the best it can be.

Poems in *Climb Inside a Poem*

"Sun and Moon: A Poem for Two Voices"
"Hidden Treasures"

Read More by Bobbi Katz

A Rumpus of Rhymes: A Book of Noisy Poems
  Dutton, 2001

Pocket Poems
  Dutton, 2004

More Pocket Poems
  Dutton, 2008

Could We Be Friends? Poems for Pals
  Mondo Publishing, 1997

Once Around the Sun
  Harcourt, 2007

Partner Poems for Building Fluency
  Scholastic, 2007

Truck Talk: Rhymes on Wheels
  Scholastic, 1997

Germs, Germs, Germs!
  Scholastic, 1996

Make Way for Tooth Decay
  Scholastic, 1999

Trailblazers: Poems of Exploration
  Greenwillow, 2007

X. J. Kennedy

"Read poems. Lots of poems. All kinds of poems . . . You'll find it becomes easier to write poems yourself."

Getting to Know X. J. Kennedy

X. J. Kennedy was born in Dover, New Jersey, in 1929. His name is really Joseph, but he decided to write under the name X. J. Kennedy so people wouldn't think he was the better-known Joe Kennedy of Massachusetts.

X. J. Kennedy's poems for children have been published in magazines such as *Cricket* and *Highlights for Children* and in anthologies. Mr. Kennedy writes for adults and children and has won many awards and honors for his writing. He has published at least eighteen books for youngsters.

X. J. Kennedy and his wife, Dorothy, live in Lexington, Massachusetts. Mr. Kennedy's wife is also a writer, and they have created several books together. They have five grown children and six grandchildren.

Poet to Poet: Tips for Young Writers

Finding Ideas for Writing

X. J. Kennedy says,

"Poems start out in different ways. Some begin when I notice something, or experience something, or think of something, or read about something that . . . sets off strong feelings. These things may be anything from a newspaper article about fireflies to the experience of blowing the fuzz from a dandelion. A poem is what happens when I'm trying to fix those things into keepable shape. But about half the time, a poem will start without any idea at all, without any special feelings. I think of a line, and it has some rhythm to it, and sounds worth keeping. Then I think up another line to rhyme with it, and the lines keep on accumulating."

Choosing the Right Tools for Writing

What are X. J. Kennedy's favorite tools for writing? He says,

"I like to write on my computer, because it's so easy to change stuff. If there isn't any computer handy, then I'll write with pen, pencil, anything, on any kind of paper that comes to hand and transfer it to my computer later."

So, poets, it sounds as if X. J. Kennedy makes many revisions since he likes the computer for changing things easily. And we know that rewriting and revisions make our writing stronger.

Advice for Young Poets

This is X. J. Kennedy's advice for young poets:

> "Try to remember the poems you read or hear. The ones you love, that is, the few that really talk to you. You can forget about the rest. But those favorite poems you discover, fix them in your head. Try saying them back again, out loud or to yourself. Make them part of you. You'll find it becomes easier to write poems yourself, maybe poems that, if you're lucky, might become favorites of other people."

We already have some favorite poems in our class. Can you think of one we have tucked away in our hearts and in our memories? Let's try to say one of our favorites aloud right now. I think X. J. Kennedy is right, that when you have poems tucked away in your heart and mind, you will write better poems too.

Poems in *Climb Inside a Poem*

"Laundromat"

Read More by X. J. Kennedy

Exploding Gravy: Poems to Make You Laugh
    Little, Brown, 2002
Elympics: Poems
    Philomel, 1999
The Beasts of Bethlehem
    Margaret K. McElderry Books, 1992
Talking Like the Rain: A Read-to-Me Book of Poems
    Little, Brown, 1992
The Kite That Braved Old Orchard Beach: Year-Round Poems for Young People
    Margaret K. McElderry, 1991
Brats
    Margaret K. McElderry, 1986
The Forgetful Wishing Well: Poems for Young People
    Atheneum, 1985
Knock at a Star: A Child's Introduction to Poetry
    Little, Brown revised edition, 1999

J. Patrick Lewis

"If you want to do a favor for a child who tells you he wants to be a writer, hand him [or her] a dictionary."

"Poetry gives the reader the 'ah-ha' experience, by which he [or she] will look at something now in a way he [or she] had never thought to do before."

Getting to Know J. Patrick Lewis

J. Patrick Lewis has three children (Beth, Matt, and Leigh Ann) and three grandchildren. He lives in Chagrin Falls, Ohio, with his wife, Susan. J. Patrick Lewis is a full-time writer who visits over 40 elementary schools each year. He has published more than 45 picture books. Thirty-six of his books are collections of children's poetry.

Mr. Lewis's poems have also appeared in *Cricket, Spider, Ladybug, Cicada, Odyssey, Ranger Rick, Highlights for Children, Ms. Magazine, Your Big Backyard, Creative Classroom, Storytime, Storyworks, Chickadee, Ahoy, Journal of Children's Literature, Bookbird,* and over 70 anthologies. He wrote the 1992 National Children's Book Week poem, printed in one million bookmarks and distributed nationally. He also reviews children's books for *The New York Times.*

To find out more about J. Patrick Lewis, visit www. jpatricklewis.com.

Poet to Poet: Tips for Young Writers

Finding Ideas for Writing

J. Patrick Lewis says his ideas begin with words and phrases that push him into new thoughts. He says that if you want to be a writer, you need to read a lot.

"In books are words, in words are ideas."

Finding the Best Place to Work

J. Patrick Lewis says,

"Writers are strange birds. They all seem to have their own odd behaviors. I have a great deal of difficulty writing anywhere but in the chair in which I now sit in a middle-class house on a middle-class street in the middle of America."

Finding Time for Writing

Some writers do work on their writing every-single-day. J. Patrick Lewis is one of them. He says,

"I am in this chair by 7 A.M. every morning I am not at school visits, and I leave it at about 5 P.M., seven days a week. If someone told me, for some reason, that I could no longer follow this pattern, I'm afraid fur would fly. Of course, by 'writing routine,' I mean that I am also sitting here reading, thinking, rewriting, thinking, rewriting . . ."

Poets, there is that advice again: spend time rewriting to make your work the best it can be.

Advice for Young Poets

What does J. Patrick Lewis recommend to young writers like you? He says,

"Read, read, read. Nothing new in that. Such advice is confirmed over several millennia."

Poems in *Climb Inside a Poem*

"School Bus Lady"
"Happy Teeth"

Read More by J. Patrick Lewis

Doodle Dandies: Poems That Take Shape
Atheneum, 1998
Good Mousekeeping: And Other Animal Home Poems
Atheneum, 2001
The Snowflake Sisters
Atheneum, 2003
Please Bury Me in the Library
Harcourt, 2005
God Made the Skunk: And Other Animal Poems
Doggerel Daze, 2005
Wing Nuts: Screwy Haiku [With Paul B. Janeczko]
Little, Brown, 2006
Good Mornin', Ms. America: The U.S.A. in Verse
School Specialty, 2006
Tulip at the Bat
Little, Brown, 2007
Big Is Big (and little, little): A Book of Contrasts
Holiday House, 2007
Under the Kissletoe: Christmastime Poems
Boyds Mills Press, 2007

Beverly McLoughland

"Poetry pays attention to the world and to our experience in the world. It can make us stop and wonder."

Getting to Know Beverly McLoughland

Beverly McLoughland fell in love with poetry when she was a child. She remembers having a big book of Mother Goose rhymes, which she read and reread till she knew them all by heart. As she grew older, she read all kinds of poems and memorized some of them, not because she was forced to, but because she loved the sound of the words so much.

She started writing poems when she was around 12 or 13, but she never thought she would become a writer. She had always wanted to be a teacher. So after she graduated from college she taught second grade for a few years, and she shared lots of poetry with her students. Then she decided she would like to be a writer, and she has been writing ever since. She has two cats that keep her company when she is writing. The cats are named Allie and Winnie.

Beverly McLoughland's poems are usually published in magazines, including *Highlights for Children*, *Ladybug*, *Cricket*, and *Spider*. She has also published a book of animal poems.

Poet to Poet: Tips for Young Writers

Finding Ideas for Writing

Beverly McLoughland says,

"Ideas for my poems come in many different ways. Many come from my sense of wonder and curiosity about animals and the natural world. The two poems in [*Climb Inside a Poem*] began that way. 'Spring Riddles' came from my amazement at how strangely nature works sometimes—that from a frog's eggs come these funny-looking tadpole-y creatures—instead of frogs! 'Night Story' came about from looking up at the stars and wondering about them."

Finding the Best Place to Work

Once Beverly McLoughland gets an idea, she has to decide where she will write. She says,

> "I usually write at the kitchen table where I sit facing the living room window. When I look up from my writing, I can see the woods, which relaxes my eyes and my mind."

When you write, are you like Beverly McLoughland? Do you find it helpful to look outside when you are thinking about what comes next in your writing?

Finding Time for Writing

Finding the time to write is a big task for writers. Some can write almost any time. Others need a big block of time to get focused and get the work of writing done. Here's how Beverly McLoughland finds time for writing.

> "I try to write regularly every day for a few hours. I'm a slow writer. I can't sit and write if I only have a few minutes. I need a big chunk of time. I don't always keep to this schedule because sometimes other things get in the way of writing. Sometimes, when a poem is really going well and I'm very excited about it, I'll stay up late at night to write. The important thing for me is to try to work as often and as regularly as I can."

Poets, think about that; Beverly McLoughland writes like we do. She has time every day that she puts aside for writing.

Poems in *Climb Inside a Poem*

"Spring Riddles"
"Night Story"

Read More by Beverly McLoughland

A Hippo's a Heap: And Other Animal Poems
Boyds Mills Press, 1993

Pat Mora

"We are all poets, and . . . each of us has songs or rhymes or stories or word pictures that we can share."

Getting to Know Pat Mora

Pat Mora was born in El Paso, Texas, which is on the border of Mexico. She grew up speaking both Spanish and English in her home. She now lives in Santa Fe, New Mexico, and is the mother of three adult children.

Pat Mora enjoys family and friend time, reading and gardening, cooking, and seeing museums and the wonders of the natural world when she travels and when she returns home to Santa Fe. Ms. Mora enjoys writing for both children and adults. She is the author of over 25 books for children. She speaks often at conferences, universities, and schools, talking about writing, family literacy, and leadership.

To find out more about Pat Mora, visit www.patmora.com.

Poet to Poet: Tips for Young Writers

Finding Ideas for Writing

Pat Mora says,

> "Poems can be responses to a specific stimulus—a scene, sound, scent, memory, melody, taste, worry. Our responses come from all *we* are too, and in this case all I am. My hope is to put myself in a receptive place, and then to play with what surfaces onto the page, like finger painting."

What a lovely idea it is to think of playing with ideas and words in our writing like we play with color and movement when we finger-paint. Did you notice that she gets ideas from scents? I wonder what idea you might get if you smelled a cake baking or breakfast cooking. Did you notice that she gets ideas from tastes? I wonder what idea you might get if you tasted watermelon or hot chocolate. It is fun to think about things like that. Maybe we could bring in some things to smell and taste or some music to listen to and see if we get ideas for writing.

Finding the Best Place to Work

Does Pat Mora have a favorite place to do her writing? She says,

> "It was so many years before I was actually able to give my writing its space, that I can scribble drafts on hotel memo pads—and have many times. I've written in places I didn't particularly like and in places I love. Time is the premium issue for me. In Santa Fe, I don't have an office but like to write at the dining room table where I can see trees and hear birds."

Even though many of us do have a favorite place to write, we know that we can't always be there when it is time to write. So, just like Pat Mora, we have to learn to write wherever we are when a good idea comes along.

Finding Time for Writing

Pat Mora speaks at many schools, and at conferences for teachers and meetings for writers, all year. She has to travel a lot in her work. So she doesn't get to sit at her dining room table in Santa Fe and write every morning. How is she able to get the work of writing done? She says,

> "If I didn't travel as much as I do, I'd tend to write in the morning and do desk work (e-mail, etc.) in the afternoon. To get the writing and revising (how I love it) DONE, I set deadlines for myself—in pencil. I don't fault myself for not always making these arbitrary goals, but they keep me moving along on what matters to me. I'm gently firm with myself, but it's not that hard since I love what I do."

That's another good idea for us to try—setting deadlines. We could make a plan when we write and decide when we think we will be able to finish. Then we can work toward that goal, just like Pat Mora does. But, we won't get upset if we aren't able to get it all done in time, just like Ms. Mora.

Poems in *Climb Inside a Poem*

"Happy Toes"
"Quack, Quack"

Read More by Pat Mora

¡Marimba!: Animales from A to Z
  Clarion, 2006
Uno, Dos, Tres: One, Two, Three
  Clarion, 1996
Confetti: Poemas para ninos | Poems for Children
  Lee & Low, 2006
The Desert Is My Mother | El Desierto Es Mi Madre
  Pinata, 1994

Doña Flor: A Tall Tale About a Giant Woman with a Great Big Heart
     Knopf, 2005
The Race of Toad and Deer
     Groundwood, 2001
Tomás and the Library Lady
     Knopf, 1997
Pablo's Tree
     Simon & Schuster, 1994
Listen to the Desert / Oye al Desierto
     Clarion reprint edition, 2001
A Birthday Basket for Tía
     Aladdin reprint edition, 1997

Alice Schertle

"Poetry speaks to the heart and to the mind. A cherished poem is a gift that we may carry with us all our lives."

Getting to Know Alice Schertle

Alice Schertle used to be an elementary-school teacher. She lived in California most of her life, but a few years ago she moved to Massachusetts. She loves writing, and when she's not writing, or spreading the word about the joys of writing and reading, she likes to tramp around the woods of New England. There, she says, "Poems whisper through the trees and flow in the streams."

Ms. Schertle once kept all three of her children home from school so that she could read a book to them. "I read them a whole novel between breakfast and dinner," she says, "with a break for lunch. My kids remember it as a great day." It was reading to her own children that renewed her love of children's books and made her want to write them.

Alice Schertle is the author of more than 40 books for children, including picture books and award-winning collections of poetry. She has won many awards for her work. Ms. Schertle says one of the few things as wonderful as reading a poem is writing one. "I find writing poetry absorbing, difficult, satisfying, frustrating, maddening, intriguing—I love it!"

To find out more about Alice Schertle, you can visit the website of her publisher and click on her name at www.harpercollinschildrens.com

Poet to Poet: Tips for Young Writers

Advice for Young Poets
Alice Schertle says,

"If you want to write poetry, read poetry."

So, poets, when you have free time, select a poem from our classroom library, or return to a favorite poem from Climb Inside a Poem, *and read it yourself. Read it over and over again so it plays like a CD in your brain. In fact, Ms. Schertle says,*

"Notice the rhythm of the words and the patterns of the lines. And never read a poem only once. You'll develop an ear for the sounds and rhythms of language almost like developing an ear for music."

Finding Ideas for Writing

Alice Schertle says that ideas for her poems come from all sorts of places:

"Images, sounds, feelings—also dreams, stories, a newspaper headline, a traffic jam, a snatch of conversation, the taste of pizza, sand in my shoe—so many things can inspire a poem. The best inspiration of all, I think, is an SSN, a Sudden Strange Notion."

Finding the Best Place to Work

Poets, when you're ready to write, what's your favorite place to work? At your desk? On the floor on a big pillow? Alice Schertle says,

"I write most often sitting at my desk. But any place that's quiet and without distractions will do. I'd love to be able to write out under a tree in the woods behind my house, but I find everything outdoors extremely distracting. I'll look at the leaves moving in the wind or an ant crawling up a weed or moss on a stone wall, and suddenly an hour has gone by and, though I've loved every minute, I haven't written a thing."

So, poets, the next time you are ready to write, think about Alice Schertle. Maybe, like her, you could try some place quiet, without distractions.

Poems in *Climb Inside a Poem*

"The Stray Dog"
"Just Like Grandpa"

Read More by Alice Schertle

Very Hairy Bear
　　Harcourt, 2007
The Adventures of Old Bo Bear
　　Chronicle, 2006
All You Need for a Snowman
　　Harcourt, 2002
Down the Road
　　Voyager reprint edition, 2000